VIDEO MARKETING FOR MARKETERS

VIDEO MARKETING
— FOR —
MARKETERS

BUILDING TRUST,
ENGAGEMENT, AND
CONVERSION ON
THE CUSTOMER
JOURNEY

ADRIAN SANDMEIER

COPYRIGHT © 2019 ADRIAN SANDMEIER
All rights reserved.

VIDEO MARKETING FOR MARKETERS
Building Trust, Engagement, and Conversion on the Customer Journey

ISBN   978-1-5445-0594-7   *Hardcover*
       978-1-5445-0592-3   *Paperback*
       978-1-5445-0593-0   *Ebook*

In memory of my mother, Erika Sandmeier

CONTENTS

FOREWORD 9
INTRODUCTION 13

ACT I: THE BASICS: GETTING READY FOR VIDEO MARKETING
1. WELCOME TO VIDEO MARKETING 31
2. TAKE INVENTORY 43
3. REALIZE YOUR POTENTIAL 67
4. STRATEGIES FOR IMPLEMENTING VIDEO 105

ACT II: LET'S GO INTO PRODUCTION
5. WHY YOU SHOULD HIRE A VIDEO PRODUCTION COMPANY 129
6. THE PREPRODUCTION PROCESS 151
7. THE PRODUCTION PROCESS 181
8. THE POST-PRODUCTION PROCESS 189

ACT III: DISTRIBUTION AND WHAT COMES NEXT
9. YOU HAVE A VIDEO: NOW WHAT? 201
10. SMART DISTRIBUTION: TRACK, MEASURE, ANALYZE, AND LEVERAGE RESULTS 221
11. TOP 15 VIDEO MARKETING MISTAKES TO AVOID 233

CONCLUSION 243
ACKNOWLEDGMENTS 247
ABOUT THE AUTHOR 251

FOREWORD

By Florian Stein, Founder and Search Engine Marketing Specialist, Werbeagentur-Erfurt.net

Over the years, I have enjoyed collaborating with youstream's founder, my friend Adrian Sandmeier, on many projects and productions from online marketing to film and, finally, video marketing.

Adrian first got into video marketing to promote his film agency in Switzerland. Within just a few months, he relaunched the company's website, and youstream was born. I've watched his business grow quickly and seen his many customers enjoy their own successes due to Adrian's expertise and the combined efforts of his production team. During this time, I shared my own insights on video marketing with Adrian and so, through my own small contributions, I proudly share in his continuing success.

Adrian's timing could not have been better. On February 14, 2005, the video search engine YouTube.com was launched, and it has since seen unprecedented growth and success in ninety-one countries worldwide. Meanwhile, this Google subsidiary has become the second largest search engine in the world with currently over 1.9 billion active monthly users. Over 400 hours of video are uploaded each minute, with 70 percent of that content being viewed on mobile devices.[1] These impressive numbers illustrate the importance of videos in our lives and the opportunities the medium has to offer companies eager to harness its power.

I've been involved with the development of online marketing in the DACH (German, Austrian, and Swiss) region since 2008, with a focus on search engine marketing. Since 2011, my team from Werbeagentur-Erfurt.net and I have worked with numerous clients to solve an important question: How can businesses create and manage a consistent stream of visitors online? It is extremely important for companies to create great content in the form of text, images, graphics, and (of course) videos to bring traffic to their websites.

Adrian's book intends to provide you with a comprehensive overview of what to look for in video production and

---

[1] Kit Smith, "52 interesting numbers and statistics about YouTube," *Brandwatch*, July 25, 2019 https://www.brandwatch.com/de/blog/statistiken-youtube/.

the subsequent video marketing measures in the context of search engine marketing. A key focus of my thoughts on successful video marketing is centered on the homepage. Related to this is another important question: How can videos be used to turn visitors into customers? Effective user guidance, SEO measures, and search engine advertising play a central role in this process. Each of these elements will be clarified throughout this book.

I hope you enjoy this book as much as I have. More importantly, I hope you consider Adrian's advice and accept his guidance so you, too, can enjoy the success enjoyed by so many who have taken their marketing and their businesses to the next level—with *video*.

INTRODUCTION

This book is for marketers who want to learn about video marketing. I wrote it because in my work as a video producer, I'm surrounded every day by marketers and business leaders who are new to video and don't know where to start. Step by step, I guide them through the process.

Many people who approach me and my team share similar challenges:

1. They are new to video marketing.
2. They are insecure about the criteria of choosing the right video marketing company.
3. They lack a clear plan.

In some cases, they have already created a plan that takes into account what they need to accomplish right now, but with no long-term strategy behind it. Nor does it correspond to their existing overall marketing strategy. What's different about the way that I teach people about video marketing is my focus on marketing and the customer journey: *there is a purpose behind everything we do, and it revolves around the customer journey.* Any good production company can make a beautiful video, but if it doesn't meet your prospects and customers where they are on their customer journey, it won't solve your marketing problems or help you achieve your goals.

In this book, you will learn how companies use video to build trust and engage with people, introduce new products, reinforce buying decisions, and convert prospects into customers. The possibilities are greater than you can imagine.

> "One factor that is common to all purchasing decisions is trust."[2]

Video marketing has been around for a few decades. Yet for many businesses, video is still uncharted territory—the unexplored frontier in marketing. Marketers know they should be using video, and they want to use it, but often they don't know where to start. They don't understand enough about it to begin, or to communicate the

---

2   Olivier Njamfa, "The importance of trust to the customer experience," *Eptica*, March 1, 2016, https://www.eptica.com/blog/importance-trust-customer-experience.

value and benefits to company leadership. To get the buy-in—and the budget—for video marketing, they need a little help.

I see this all the time working with businesses at my company. Since I started producing videos for business owners and marketers more than a decade ago, I've learned that, with the right strategy, any business can benefit from video marketing. If you finish this book and make the move to add video to your marketing strategy, a lot will change. The way you communicate with your customers and how they view you and respond to you will never be the same.

You're probably well aware of the value and benefits of video marketing. A little research shows that video is the most exciting thing to happen to marketing since the internet. Consider the facts:

- Seventy-two percent of consumers prefer video over text marketing.[3]
- Companies that use video experience a 41 percent increase in traffic through web searches.[4]

---

3 Dan Alaimo, "72% of consumers prefer videos to text marketing," *Retail Dive*, May 23, 2018, https://www.retaildive.com/news/72-of-consumers-prefer-videos-to-text-marketing/524161/.

4 William Craig, "The Growth of Video Marketing and Why Your Business Needs It," *Forbes*, April 24, 2018, https://www.forbes.com/sites/williamcraig/2018/04/24/the-growth-of-video-marketing-and-why-your-business-needs-it/#13b533de7c2d.

- Fifty-nine percent of executives prefer video over text.[5]
- Ninety-two percent of mobile video consumers share videos.[6]
- Social video generates twelve times the shares of text and images combined.[7]

If you're not using video, it's time to start. Use it to introduce people to your company, products, and services. Use it to build rapport with your target audience and develop a following of customers who are loyal to your products and devoted to your brand. With enough insight, you can add video to your marketing mix and begin reaping the benefits of this groundbreaking medium in just a few months.

In this book, I'll tell you what video marketing is and why and how to use it to build trust with your audience, get them to engage with you, and convert them to loyal customers at each phase of their customer journey. I'll give you all the guidance you need to design a video marketing plan you can communicate to your leadership and your team that gets everyone on board with this amazing marketing platform.

---

[5] Matt Mansfield, "27 Video Marketing Statistics That Will Have You Hitting the Record Button," *Small Business Trends*, January 16, 2019, https://smallbiztrends.com/2016/10/video-marketing-statistics.html.

[6] "27 Video Marketing Statistics That Will Have You Hitting the Record Button."

[7] "27 Video Marketing Statistics That Will Have You Hitting the Record Button."

UNTANGLING THE MYTHS AROUND VIDEO

Confusion around video marketing causes some marketers to hesitate or avoid using it altogether. They think it's too hard or too expensive. While it can be expensive, with the right strategy they could be using video to separate themselves from the competition and make it pay off. If they knew more about video, they'd stop waiting and start doing it. They just need someone to untangle the misconceptions from the truth and demystify the process. I'm here to do just that.

Video marketing isn't as simple as some of the marketing media you're currently using. It comprises many moving pieces—story, rhythm, sound, visuals, narration, emotion, and more—and demands more from you, but those demands are *exactly* what make video such a powerful force in your content strategy. Working with a production team, you'll identify your target audience, locate their position on the customer journey, and determine the right message to deliver.

"Video is an emotional medium, perfect for connecting with potential customers and standing out in a crowded field of competitors."[8]

---

8   Hope Horner, "How Video Can Help You Build Relationships and Trust With Your Customers," *Inc.*, https://www.inc.com/young-entrepreneur-council/how-to-build-relationships-and-trust-with-your-customers-through-video.html.

You'll do some soul-searching to ensure your message truly reflects your company—who you are and what you stand for. That authenticity is what makes you stand out for your audience and helps them decide if they want to engage with you.

Through distribution, measuring, and analytics, you'll learn a lot about your customers, too, and you can use that insight to improve your products, services, and your video marketing strategy. For starters, you can count every time a customer clicks on your video, track when they stop watching it, and connect those customers and views to specific calls to action. No other marketing medium allows this degree of targeted granularity, interaction, communication, and engagement between you and your customers.

Years ago, you needed a sizable budget to produce and distribute a video. Channels were limited, so you couldn't pick and choose who you reached or how you reached them. Today, anyone can put a video on YouTube or on their own website. Even more powerful, you can pay to have your video placed exactly where your target audience spends time. Meanwhile, you can analyze how well your video is performing and set next steps to continuously improve your campaign. This wasn't even possible two decades ago!

Easy access to social media channels allows you to reach

people around the world while they're waiting for an appointment or during their commute times, on their mobile phones, tablets, laptops, desktops, and TVs. These opportunities level the playing field for businesses of all sizes and open the door for small- to mid-size companies to grow faster than ever before.

"Fifty percent of executives look for more information after seeing a product or service in a video. In fact, 65 percent of them visit the marketer's website and 39 percent call a vendor after viewing a video."[9]

Some marketers don't use video yet because they didn't have the chance to learn about it in school. Video marketing wasn't taught in marketing degree programs in the past, and in many colleges, it still hasn't been introduced. You can wait for the textbooks to be written and for universities to begin implementing video programs, or you can learn about it with a little research, beginning with this book.

While your competitors hesitate, you can start using video marketing and still be ahead of the curve. Using it gives you the advantage, instead of relying on older marketing methods that put you at a disadvantage against other businesses.

---

9   "27 Video Marketing Statistics That Will Have You Hitting the Record Button."

Video marketing has changed exponentially since I made my first video, and it's evolving more *quickly* each day. Software and hardware improvements and technological advances like AI have increased the mobility, speed, ease of access, and ability of video to adapt to people's changing behaviors and allowed it to break through the filters that leave other marketing platforms behind. It has completely altered the way companies interact with their customers, and it's not going away.

MY LIFE IN VIDEO

I started in video more than a decade ago and was fortunate to have some very talented mentors along the way—people I interacted with in the industry and whose work I studied in books and by watching videos.

In Switzerland, I met Andreas Schneider, a graduate of the prestigious Ernst Busch Academy of Dramatic Arts in Berlin. Speaking with Andreas, I was surprised by all the nuances acting can bring to video and film— the emotion it can transmit and stories you can build with a tactical approach. I couldn't wait to learn more and was eager to work on a project with him. Andreas was doing radio and TV at the time, and I soon discovered that he wasn't very interested in the scriptwriting side, so if we were going to work together, I had to start writing. I took classes in renowned film schools in Hamburg and Munich to prepare, and we created two short films and some image, or *brand*, films for companies. That experience both fascinated me and introduced me to many aspects of filmmaking such as acting, dialogue, and many other details that are essential to video.

I'll never forget when our first project appeared on a film festival's short list. After several days of teamwork, putting in long hours, our work was actually being recognized! Sitting among the audience—watching the film and thinking about how we had turned an idea into an entire *movie*—felt like a miracle. This was the turning point that reaffirmed what I knew in my heart: I had to learn more, produce more, and create more videos. Ultimately, that experience drove me to pursue a career in video production and marketing.

I got my first real job in video as a technician for a large broadcaster covering entertainment and sports. Working out of an OB (outside broadcasting) van, I traveled to hundreds of national and international events, including the 2014 Winter Olympics in Sochi. Everything had to go right the first time on those shoots, because there was no second chance. The colors had to be matched, the sound leveled, and all the video signals at the right place. *Everything* had to be perfect—so preparation was key. With no do-overs, I learned fast.

I enjoyed learning all the technical aspects of video production, but was fascinated by the creative side, too. So in Germany, I continued to study scriptwriting and refined my dialogue writing skills. I cast and produced several short films and found that leading video productions came naturally to me, so I began working independently with companies on image videos. Experience taught me that the magic of video was in the people and the stories they shared. This remains the common thread throughout all of my video production: *it's always about the people and the nuances that communicate authenticity.*

While working in television production, I had begun building my own business, and by 2015, I was running my own full-service video production company. Since then, I've produced hundreds of videos for my customers that have been viewed from tens of thousands to millions of times. In the chapters that follow, I'll describe some of these projects and the thought process, planning, and production that went into them.

YOUR GUIDE TO VIDEO MARKETING

You've read this far, because as a marketer or business leader, you know the potential of video marketing and want to begin using it to build your business's brand, products, and services. This book is your guide to help you connect with your target audience, build trust and engagement, and convert potential customers to loyal customers.

This is not a guide for video students or production professionals who want to learn the latest techniques in scriptwriting, production, and editing. I could teach you those skills, but they are subjects for another book. Instead, I will show you how to *choose* the right production company for your video marketing. My goal is for you to become a better marketer by learning how to up your marketing game with video and get the kinds of results you can't get with any other marketing medium.

I'll teach you about video marketing in a way that will help you explain it to your colleagues, your team, and your leadership. Unless you're a sole proprietor, you will need their support to get your video marketing project off the ground. You'll need to help your team and company decision-makers understand the concepts, processes, and value of video marketing in order to get their buy-in and bring them enthusiastically on board.

"Businesses using video grow company revenue 49 percent faster year-over-year than organizations without video."[10]

---

10 "27 Video Marketing Statistics That Will Have You Hitting the Record Button."

By the time you're done reading, you'll be prepared to make the right video marketing decisions for your business. You'll have a clear path with all the steps you need to take on the way.

VIDEO MARKETING IN THREE ACTS

I wrote this book in three acts to prepare you for the process of working with a video production company and to show you what to do with your video after it's completed.

Act I, *The Basics: Getting Ready for Video Marketing,* lays the foundation for your video marketing adventure. It provides a summary of how consumer buying habits and viewing trends have changed, so you know where we came from and how we got here. You'll see how video marketing has altered the trajectory of buying decisions, how entrenched video has become in the customer journey, and how to use this to your advantage to build trust with your audience, engage with them, and convert them to customers.

Act I also teaches you what to do before you move forward with video marketing. At some point you'll contact a video production company. Act I covers what you need to do *before* that moment. It prepares you with questions to ask yourself and actions to take prior to approaching production. Think of this as a journey—your video marketer's journey. Before you take a trip, you have to know why you're going on the trip. You have to know where you're going, what you're going to do when you get there, and how to pack. It's the same with your journey into video marketing, and I will be here to guide you from start to finish.

In this first act, we'll take inventory of where you are right now. You may have problems with your current marketing channels such as your website and social media sites or your video platforms like YouTube. We'll talk about how to solve those problems so your channels and platforms are in top shape to host your video.

We'll also talk about your current content strategy and how video fits in. If you don't have a content strategy, including guidelines around how your company uses text and images and how you communicate with your customers, you will need to make those decisions before beginning a video.

If you've had a formal marketing education or extensive marketing experience, some of this will be familiar to you, but if you came into a position in marketing without any training and have been learning as you go, expect a steeper learning curve. Regardless of your previous experience, you will learn how video works and how you can incorporate it into your marketing content strategy.

In Act I, I'll also introduce the various marketing channels available to you. I'll show you how they work and discuss different strategies for implementing video in each of them.

Act II, *Let's Go Into Production,* covers what happens after you've decided to move forward with your first video production. We'll discuss your first decision in the production process: to do all the work in-house, hire a consultant, or team up with a video production company. I will teach you how to select a company and how to prepare for your first meeting. Proper communication with your video producers is key to getting the video—and the results—you want and expect.

In this act, I'll step you through the production plan, including preproduction, production, and post-production—every stage in the process of creating a video concept and bringing the script to final edit. Your goals, messaging, budget, and distribution strategy are all important considerations, as well as your target audience and their location on the customer journey. We'll do a deep dive into how the story you tell in video defines your business and your message.

Act III, *Distribution and What Comes Next,* explores what happens after you've made your video. Here you will learn the details of putting your distribution plan into play to ensure that your video is seen and potential customers are moved to take action. We'll discuss analytics and key measurements such as impressions, click rates, and conversions—how to track them, improve them, and use what you learn to advance your business.

Video marketing is the most exciting development in marketing since the internet. Prepare to learn how you can leverage the power of video to change how you interact with customers in new and exciting ways. In the pages that follow, you'll be on your way to making a dramatic difference in how you talk to your customers and how they respond.

I guarantee that you'll never look at marketing the same way again.

Are you ready to start? We'll begin with a look at how the power of video has changed the world. You're about to learn how you can harness its power to change your business.

ACT I

THE BASICS: GETTING READY FOR VIDEO MARKETING

CHAPTER 1

WELCOME TO VIDEO MARKETING

Video marketing has many definitions. In this book, it's described as "a resource for reaching your business goals." Video is the only medium that combines written and spoken words, graphics, music, form, color, light, movement, message, story, action, drama, and emotions into a form of communication that can be accessed at any time and from almost anywhere in the world.

Video marketing communicates your company's value to your target audience. It connects you with your current customers and people who want to be your customers. Everything you do with video marketing—from identifying your target audience, crafting the right message, and producing the video to distributing it and measuring the results—is about that connection.

Video marketing by itself will not solve all your marketing needs. It's most effective when applied within the context of your marketing master plan. Video is arguably the most powerful medium for transmitting content, but it is just one part of your overall content strategy.

Despite the power of video, companies miss out on its power by neglecting to use it anywhere, including the most obvious place—their websites. Take a look at your company website and the websites of your competitors. Many rely on text, images, and photographs to communicate with their audiences. Worse, a lot of sites still use stock images instead of their own photos or artwork, which is a missed opportunity to communicate authenticity.

Companies avoid using video for a lot of reasons. The main reason is their lack of experience and awareness. They don't even know how to get started. The typical marketer doesn't understand the cost or the effort involved, and they don't know how to measure the results. Some marketers are simply afraid of doing it wrong, which is understandable if you've never done it before. But with the right preparation and strategy, you can design a video marketing plan that's within your budget and meets your business goals.

WHY VIDEO

People love video. Teens and adults spend more time watching YouTube videos than television broadcast shows.[11] When given the choice between reading text and watching video, people usually choose video because it transmits content faster. It combines voice, sound, and moving pictures to transmit much more in less time than other marketing media. Unlike radio or podcasts, where viewers hear your message with their ears, or print media or text, where they see it with their eyes, video is experienced through sight and sound for a richer cognitive experience.

"A one-minute video is worth 1.8 million words."[12]

New clients often come to me because their competitors are using video, so they think they should be using it too. This isn't a bad reason, but it is reactive, and waiting for your competitors to "go first" isn't necessary—you don't have to wait. You *shouldn't* wait. The sooner you start, the sooner you'll begin building your audience, getting to know them by analyzing their behavior, and allow-

---

[11] Kelton Global, "Younger Viewers Watch 2.5 Times More Internet Video Than TV," *KeltonGlobal.com*, March 29, 2016, https://www.keltonglobal.com/recognition/younger-viewers-watch-2-5-times-more-internet-video-than-tv/.

[12] James L. McQuivey, "How Video Will Take Over the World," *Forrester.com*, June 17, 2008, https://www.forrester.com/report/How+Video+Will+Take+Over+The+World/-/E-RES44199#.

ing them to get to know you in a way you've never done before.

Video transmits the culture of your company to the public, and it changes your company culture. When you make your company more visible, and you include your employees in video, you are engaging your employees in what your company stands for. For this reason, it's a good idea to consider how job candidates feel about video when you're hiring new people. You will want to include as many staff members in the video as you can, and so the more enthusiastic they are about it, the better. Consider adding language in your hiring contracts letting new employees know that you use video marketing. You might also include a model release form for them to sign, so that if they appear in a video, you can use it while they're employed and if they leave, too.

THE ADVANTAGES

Video marketing allows you to differentiate yourself in how you present your business to the audience you want to reach. It separates you from the competition, whether they're using video or not. It allows you to target customers at a very granular level. By evaluating your goals and value proposition, analyzing your desired audience, and developing specific "persona" profiles of the people you want to reach, you can create content that reaches the right people in order to achieve your business goals. This is important, because people are subjected to a lot of media "noise"—marketing that they have to get past to find the messages they're looking for.

You can communicate your value proposition to your audience, but more than that, you can share your culture. Every choice you make for your videos conveys a message that tells your prospects and customers if your company is for them or not. It shows them what your business and the people who work there care about. Video shows people what you believe in and what you have to offer to make their lives better. It can evoke emotion, nurture trust, and create a bond between you. Video marketing creates a sense of togetherness and promotes loyalty between you and your customers.

The enhanced power of connecting with people is one advantage of video marketing, but it can also be used for branding your business. By using the same color palette, graphics, narrators, characters, music, logos, and even font in your videos, you familiarize yourself to your audience. They get to know you and recognize you immediately. This is another reason that video marketing should be part of your content strategy—a style guide for all your other marketing content can be reflected in your production, amplifying your brand and the power of your marketing campaigns.

With video, you can tell an emotional, memorable story that sticks with the viewer. You can also include a call to action with written and verbal contact details and directions on what to do next. Calls to action can be placed at the end of the video or sprinkled throughout the video.

Video stays in your long-term memory better than other media. Jim Kwik, who is a world expert on memory improvement and optimal brain performance, notes, "Information combined with emotion becomes a long-term memory."[13] When you do this with video—deliver content while evoking an emotional response—you create a potent combination that stays with a person. Information on its own will be remembered for a while, but if you add emotion through story, music, or imagery, it lingers in the viewer's memory. Think about your own most vivid memories from years past. Why do certain events remain in your memory while others drift away? They stick because *they are bound to emotion.* You were feeling something—happiness, sadness, compassion, irritation, hopefulness, worry, *something*—during those moments. It's the same with video. Your viewers will remember what you tell them when you wrap your message in an emotional story.

Another advantage of video marketing is that it's mea-

---

13 Jim Kwik, "Kwik Brain 001: Learn Anything Faster," *JimKwik.com*, March 30, 2017, https://jimkwik.com/kwik-brain-001/.

surable. A simple test of your website statistics with and without video can tell you a lot about its effectiveness—how many visits and unique visitors you have and how long they stay on your page during a set period of time. Look at how many engage and how many conversions you have. Then add video and measure the statistics again.

Video is one of the most important ratings boosters on Google, because the search engine rates website with video higher and it will also rate sites higher if people stay on them longer.

CUSTOMERS DON'T SHOP LIKE THEY USED TO

The popularity and success of video marketing didn't happen by accident. People today are expected to make decisions much faster than we used to, and video helps us make those decisions quickly. Think about how much time you spent, years ago, researching a big purchase like an appliance, car, or even a home. You might have taken time off from work to meet a salesperson, and they'd show you all the homes on the market or let you test drive any car on the lot. Today you can go online and find out everything you need to know before you buy. For many items, you can make your purchase online and have everything delivered to your front door.

Along with all this *useful* knowledge that's now available

at our fingertips is an overwhelming amount that we don't need—*noise*—so we put up filters to guard against it. We might do this consciously, but often we do it unconsciously. And we keep out people we don't trust. By using video to build trust with your customers, you are less likely to be filtered out and more likely to be let in—and considered in customers' buying decisions. The key is building trust without *adding* to the noise. This is where a video professional can help with your strategy and message.

> "The intimacy of a video marketing campaign makes it uniquely well-suited to building trust."[14]

Recently, a prospective customer in the entertainment industry came to me who needed help with his company's video campaign. Building trust with his customers was important, and he knew what he wanted his video to say to establish that trust. I was excited to work with someone with such a clear vision. So when I visited the company's website for the first time, I was a bit shocked. Nothing about it communicated trust. Whoever landed on the page had to choose from a list of thirty options to get to the next page!

Forcing people to make so many choices causes decision

---

14 Joe Forte, "5 Strategies for Building Brand Trust Through Video," *Business.com*, June 20, 2018, https://www.business.com/articles/build-trust-with-video-marketing/.

fatigue, and instead of driving them to trust you, it drives them away. If someone lands on your page, you've done something right to get them there. You have to respect their time and attention by making it easy for them to get to know you right away so they can decide to engage with you.

On this prospective customer's site, instead of squandering that attention, the company could have drawn people in with a video. They could have told a story about who they are, transmitted authenticity and honesty, and shown their culture and their brand. With the right quality, tone, message, and authenticity, they could have made an instant connection with their target audience—instead of expecting them to choose between dozens of options before they could move forward.

EVALUATING THE COST VS. THE VALUE OF VIDEO MARKETING

Small- to mid-sized companies worry about the cost of video. They may be used to paying someone one hundred dollars to write 500 words of text, while a video could cost them many times that amount. You have to evaluate the immediate and residual benefits of video to appreciate its true value.

People have stopped reading websites. Today people

scan websites. A video has the power to grab people's attention and engage them for seconds or minutes, as long as they identify a connection between themselves and the video's message. In the online world, engaging a potential customer for a few seconds or a minute is an accomplishment.

If you use a multichannel strategy and place different videos or variations of a video on your website, YouTube, and Facebook, you can measure the results and push those that have more engagement or conversions. This ability gets you to your marketing goals faster than using another medium that doesn't offer such immediate feedback or the ability to adjust to your audience response so quickly.

Video allows you to transmit your company's culture and build trust. Adding faces and authentic stories to your video makes them more real to customers and encourages feelings of trust. You can show emotion and invoke emotion in your viewer.

THE VIDEO MARKETING MINDSET

The decision to use video marketing requires a change in mindset and sometimes a change in your company's culture. It means making it part of your company's mission to communicate—not only faster, or more visually, or with more audio—but to communicate *trust*, specifically. It means being honest and sometimes vulnerable, because you have to show your "face" to many people.

Some people are comfortable getting in front of the camera. Others are ready to learn about it, and still others are completely shy about it. You can't force people to be comfortable on video or open about putting their business out there, but you can learn about the importance of communicating trust to your customers. If you understand that (and as a marketer, I'm sure you do) and understand the power of video in communicating trust, you can begin to see why it's so critical to explore the possibilities. If you decide to use video marketing for the long term—and do it right—you are also deciding to grow your culture by showing your face and your drive, sharing your thoughts, and baring your soul to your audience. That is how you build trust with them. It's what will make them want to engage with you and become your customers.

If this sounds confusing and difficult, I get it. Chances are, much of this is new to you. That's why you need a video production expert to guide you through the process.

PRINCIPLES

1. Use video to transmit trust.
2. Always communicate authentically.

TIPS

1. Always produce value for your customers in your videos. Teach them something—give them something to think about. Move them; inform them; teach, inspire, and motivate them. Don't just talk about yourself.
2. Always keep the goal in mind.
3. Video affects your company's culture. Involve your coworkers, employees, and leadership in your productions.

CHAPTER 2

TAKE INVENTORY

You know what video marketing can do for you, but before you invest in a production, lock in your marketing basics. The best way to start is with an overall plan for your future content such as text, pictures, and, of course, video. Your content strategy defines how you are going to communicate with your customers and therefore reach your business goals. It defines how often you will communicate, the channels through which you will communicate, and the role video will play. Content *marketing*—including your positioning, content strategy, viable channels such as a solid website, and other assets—needs to be in place to support your video strategy.

Companies often come to me without any marketing basics. This is common with small businesses and startups that haven't had a chance to fully develop their marketing teams or strategies. That's okay—you can still do video, but you will need to do a few other things first. You might have to hire a marketing specialist to join your company, or you could outsource the marketing. You could find a full-service video production company that will work with you on the marketing piece. Just make sure that whomever you hire understands video and its place in your marketing mix.

Don't skip this part. Too many companies skip marketing basics because they're excited to make a video—the fun stuff—and don't want to do the boring homework first. Taking inventory and getting your marketing foundation in place will pay off exponentially, not only in video but in all of your marketing endeavors.

POSITIONING

Before we get into the details of content strategy, let's be clear on what you need to know first: your *positioning*. In the words of advertising tycoon David Ogilvy, positioning is "what a product does, and who it is for." In other words, let's talk now about your UVP, *the specific value your product or service brings to your customers*, and then *who it is for*. What does your target audience look like?

When I meet with business owners and marketers for the first time and ask them to describe their products and their target markets to me in a minute or less, roughly half can't do it. They try, but they're usually not very clear or succinct. Either they don't tell me enough, and I don't understand the value of their product for the customer, or they tell me too much, and the value isn't clear.

Positioning refers to what you have to offer and who you're offering it to. It's the value of your products and services to your target audience.

YOUR UNIQUE VALUE PROPOSITION (UVP)

Your value proposition says what's unique about your product and why that uniqueness matters to the person you created it for. In other words, what value is promised to be delivered.

The key to a successful UVP is setting yourself apart from the competition. Make sure that you stand out. Communicate what value you can deliver that others cannot. It should be *relevant* to your offerings and *specific*. You can even invent a new category in your field to name yourself the first, the best, or the fastest in a certain area. Doing this will clarify your positioning and ensure powerful video messaging.

YOUR TARGET AUDIENCE

To position your company, you have to identify your target

audience—your ideal customers. The key to targeting an audience is to be as clear and specific as possible. If your company appears to be for *everybody*, it will be perceived as being for *nobody*.

To define your target audience, look at who your current ideal customers are right now. Get to know them and find out why they consume your products. What do they think is so special about you? You can ask them directly with surveys, do marketing studies, or hire a marketing company to figure this out for you. If you have more than one product, you could have more targets. That's fine—just know who they are.

Go deep with your targets and find out as much as you can about them. You can even create personas of your target groups. A persona is basically a fictional customer that you create with very specific characteristics. When you create a persona, include demographics such as their age, where they live, what kind of work they do, their income, their family situation, and what matters to them and why. When I create a persona, I even include their problems because people usually look for a service or product to solve a problem. The more specific you get with your personas, the easier it will be to create a video script that speaks to them.

It's more important for you to be aware of your prospects and customers than it is for them to be aware of you. Why? Because every penny you spend to reach the wrong audience—potentially thousands of dollars—is a waste of your precious marketing budget!

Once you've identified your target audience, you can position your company to reach *them*. Remember that people are exposed to so much on the internet; they can suffer from decision fatigue—another reason you have to make it easy for them to make up their minds about you. Proper positioning makes the greatest impact and separates you from your competition.

Figure out your positioning and then create a content strategy.

CONTENT STRATEGY AND GUIDELINES: DECIDE WHAT YOU WANT TO LOOK, SOUND, AND FEEL LIKE—THEN BE CONSISTENT

Your content strategy defines how you communicate with your audience. It comprises the words, colors, images, photographs, typography, fonts, logos, taglines, music style, narrators, movement, infographics, and any other assets that brand your business and make it identifiable. You can have values that define your company and its culture in your content strategy, tones that show your company as progressive or steady and reliable, and attitudes that show your company as authentic, serious, playful, funny, charming, respectful, or rebellious. Maybe one of your values is that the customer always comes first, and you can ensure that value is always communicated in your videos by including it in your content strategy. Your content may include certain words, and if you use those same words throughout all your marketing, your audience will begin to associate them with your business.

A WORD ABOUT WORDS

A word about words: choose them carefully. Use words your audience uses, not corporate jargon that they don't understand. That just alienates people. Think about the words you use to describe your product and how those words impact your audience. People have emotional responses to words.

Also, don't assume people know what the words you choose mean. One business I worked with wanted to use the word "fashionistas" in their video, which is a fine word that described the target group well. The problem was, many people in that group didn't know what the word meant! For some, it actually had negative connotations. If in doubt, test the words you'll use before you commit to them and add them to your style guide or content strategy.

You might have rules in your strategy, such as "never use stock footage" or "always use high-quality audio." One company that I work with has a rule that all their videos are shot at eye level. They never show people from above or below their faces. Other companies have a strategy of using many infographics to explain things, rather than text or audio. This doesn't mean they eliminate text and audio from their videos, just that they rely heavily on infographics in all their marketing to communicate, especially where it has the greatest potential for impact. The rules you put into your content strategy can even extend to details in your video production, such as "always shoot in natural light," "make every video fast-paced," or "always edit with hard cuts—no fades."

Within your content strategy, you might have a style guide that defines all your fonts and colors. Put some research into this before making these choices, because fonts and colors communicate different messages. Standard fonts like Arial and Helvetica could communicate that your company and its products are standard, too. If you're in a creative field, your content strategy should communicate that.

You might think people don't notice things like fonts and colors, or that they don't make assumptions about your company based on them, but they do—often subconsciously. There's a reason some corporations pay hundreds of thousands of dollars and more to have their own unique fonts designed by a recognized type designer.

YOUR STYLE GUIDE: BRAND YOUR BUSINESS

A style guide allows different contributors to create content in a united way that reflects your company's individual style. It ensures consistency from writing to design, saving you time and money while defining your brand—visually, through sound and motion, and other ways—so customers can identify it immediately now and in the future. Create a style guide, and your video producer (and anyone else who is involved with your content production) will love you for it! At the *very least* include these in your style guide:

- Logos: different sizes and formats for various media and backgrounds
- Fonts: static, and how they move in animated video
- Colors: your primary, secondary, and contrast colors
- Icons and symbols
- Proportions and guidelines for each marketing medium

Over time, add video-specific direction to your style guide, such as motion principles. These include visual and creative aspects for all your graphics, intros and outros, "lower thirds," music and sound effects, tonalities, camera angles, color grading, and cuts. You can get as detailed with this as you like. Some companies hire a sound creator to make their own unique sounds!

Your content strategy doesn't have to be a whole book. It can be just a few pages. But having one will help you create a video that communicates the right message to the right people.

YOUR CONTENT STRATEGY: LESS IS MORE

You don't need a hundred-page content strategy. The more focused and concise you can be, the easier it will be for you to implement it and for your audience to connect with it. Start with these questions:

- How does my content connect with my audience?
- What tonalities do I use?
- How can I create smart content that engages people?
- When do I use text, pictures, infographics, and, of course, video?
- How often do I create new content?
- Which channels do I use?
- How do I measure it?

You can use all of these in your video productions to help strengthen your company's brand.

Some companies have very detailed branding strategies. For example, Swiss International Air Lines commercials and online videos always look a certain way because they have very detailed and clear motion principles. They have their own sound creator. If you're a marketer at the company, you use the sound creator to make the right audio for all your videos.

> "The main goal of content strategy is to use words and data to create unambiguous content that supports meaningful, interactive experiences."[15]

Content strategy is especially important for the long term. It gives your videos a sense of continuity and consistency and provides your audience with a familiarity that builds trust. Before you plan your video, you should have your content marketing ready with, at the minimum, a style guide for all your marketing. You might also create a style guide specific to video that defines your intros (initial seconds of your video), outros (final seconds of your video), video graphics, and logos and their motion principles. You might decide to include your logo in all your thumbnails so that your audience sees it before they even view the video. These practices will help you be recognized faster, and customers will be able to find you and engage with you more quickly. Consistency also makes you appear

---

15 Rachel Lovinger, "Content Strategy: The Philosophy of Data," *Boxes and Arrows*, March 27, 2007, http://boxesandarrows.com/content-strategy-the-philosophy-of-data/.

more professional, and that sense of quality transfers to your products and services.

"Content strategy guides planning for the creation, delivery, and governance of useful, usable content."[16]

During preproduction, ask your production team to provide you with templates for the intro, outro, titles, and lower subtitles. Even if you switch production companies, you can take these graphic templates with you so the next producers and editors can replicate the look and feel of your earlier productions. Also talk to your production people about motion principles and ask them for advice. Get these into your first video, and the next ones will be a lot easier.

Once you've defined your content strategy, you can use it in all of your marketing collateral. This saves you money in the long run because whoever designs your collateral, advertising, newsletters, and website won't have to start from scratch.

---

[16] Kristina Halvorson and Melissa Rach, *Content Strategy for the Web* (2nd edition), Berkeley: New Riders, 2012.

CONTENT STRATEGY EXAMPLE: UPSCALE CHILD SAFETY SEAT MANUFACTURER

This example will give you a feel for creating your own content strategy. How deep you want to go is up to you. The more time and effort you put in your content marketing, the more specific your content strategy can be. Most important is that it is clear and doesn't leave any questions for your content creators.

To determine your content strategy, begin by asking yourself the following questions. The sample responses provided are for an upscale child safety seat manufacturer. This gives you an idea of how a typical content strategy is developed.

What is the **overall goal** of our content?

- Our content creates a connection with our audience.
- Our content helps our audience and delivers value.
- Our content is professional and consistent in its tonality.

Which are the **key topics** of our content?

- Safety
- Functionality
- Design

*What are the **key messages, wording, and tone** of our content?*

- Kids love our safety seats.
- Our wording is always positive. We don't scare people or use words like "accident." The focus is on how we design a high-quality safety seat and help provide a safe world for children.
- Our tone is that of a friend: we are here to help and advise parents.

What type of content *do we produce?*

- Blog with pictures and infographics
- Video content

*What is our **target group**?*

- Upper-class and affluent parents who care about status and the safety of their children.

*What **problems** does the target group encounter?*

- They need a seat for their children that is safe, functional, and of the highest quality and design.

*On which **channels** can I find my target group?*

- Website: Prospective customers find us by searching the web. They typically land on our blog or discover an ad on Google shopping (AdWords and Google Merchant Center).
- Instagram and Facebook: Paid ads on social media drive traffic to our website and landing pages.

*How exactly do we create **value** with content?*

- We give people tips and pointers about child safety.
- We educate them about the great functionality available in the latest seat designs.
- Our content does not always have to be directly related to our products.

*What is our **consistency** required to meet our goals, and what is the **budget** required to meet that consistency?*

- We need to produce fifteen blogs a month at one hundred dollars per blog, so we need a budget of $1,500 a month and $18,000 annually.
- We need to produce two videos a month at $2,500 per video, so we need a budget of $5,000 a month and $60,000 annually.

How do we measure, what do we measure, and how often do we measure *to understand the effectiveness of our content?*

- We analyze the results monthly.
- We look at the popularity of topics and responses by demographic and by geographic location.
- We use A/B testing when and where it makes sense to do so and is within the budget.

*What is included in the **style guide** for our content?*

- Logos
- Primary and secondary colors
- Fonts
- Key visuals
- Image, photograph, and infographic guidelines
- Motion principles for video

YOUR MOST IMPORTANT CHANNEL (SURPRISE! IT'S NOT SOCIAL MEDIA OR YOUTUBE)

Marketers have a vast choice of channels where they can promote their brand, products, and services. Obvious ones include the various social media channels, video platforms like YouTube, the customer newsletter, national and regional TV channels, and more. The list goes on! I even consider personal networking a channel, because you're communicating with people verbally and handing out your business card.

New channels appear while others lose their importance

among certain groups, and the momentum of each one fluctuates over time. With all these choices, a marketer can lose their way when it comes to the importance and priority of each channel. So where to start your video marketing?

Instead of getting distracted, prioritize your most important channel: your website! Think about it. *Your website is where people convert from prospects to customers.* It's typically your first touch point with customers who search for you online, and it's where you drive people through all your marketing activities. It's your website that houses all your marketing collateral and where people often make a decision to contact you or buy from you—*conversion*. It's the place where many of them will hit the "order" button and make a purchase. Done right, your website offers prospects and customers myriad ways to connect with you, and for you to connect with them. There, they will learn about you and connect with you via contact form, email, chat, or phone.

CHANNELS AND PLATFORMS

The words *channel* and *platform* are often used interchangeably in video marketing. To avoid confusion, I use these definitions in this book:

- **Channel**: Where you place your video content. This includes your website, email, social media like Facebook or Instagram, and video platforms such as YouTube and Vimeo.
- **Platform**: A channel made especially for video placement such as YouTube, Vimeo, or Wistia.

When you're working on your marketing resources, don't skimp on your website quality and improvement. It's your most important channel. Make sure that all your current and future channels reflect your content strategy with the fonts, colors, and other features you've chosen to represent your company. Your website should be up-to-date technically, too, and not created with a cheap template that gives it a clunky or dated look and feel. It should be professionally designed and easy to navigate, and it should transmit your message—what you do and whom you do it for—within five seconds. Yes, you read right: *five seconds!* Because visitors to your site *scan*. They do not read. And if they can't immediately figure out that yours is the company they're looking for, they will quickly move on.

There are many factors to consider when it comes to your website's quality, performance, and search engine rankings. Describing them all could fill an entire book, but I'm asking you to consider my personal top three. Getting *just these three things* right can have a dramatic effect on your most important marketing channel, your website: 1) performance, 2) design, and 3) SEO.

PERFORMANCE

Whether your website loads two seconds faster or slower makes a huge difference, mainly for two reasons: First, Google ranks your website's performance lower if it loads more slowly. And second, visitors to your site are impatient and might click away from your site rather than wait two full seconds. That can mean the difference between a prospect and a customer.

Typically, the problem lies with slow web servers and large, uncompressed data files that take too long to load. Make sure your servers are up-to-date and running on the latest web platforms. Check whether they are fast enough to respond to your site's traffic. You might even consider using a CDN (Content Delivery Network) if you're experiencing especially high traffic issues.

To help you gain insight into your site's performance, Google has a great tool called PageSpeed Insights, located at developers.google.com/speed/pagespeed/insights, that lets you know the exact situation with your website. It even gives you specific pointers on how to start improving, such as getting a faster server, compressing your pictures, or utilizing better coding. It also makes a distinction between mobile and desktop users, so when you are in a B2B business where prospects typically browse on their desktop, you know where to set the priorities. Use this tool to measure your website's speed and work to bring its performance into the green zone.

DESIGN

In a 2017 podcast, freelancer.com CEO Matt Barrie unveiled that after upgrading his website to a better design, his revenue doubled! The former website had been created by a few Ukrainian programmers who weren't design-savvy. Barrie then collaborated with a designer in New York and voilà—instant revenue boost.[17] Never underestimate what a well-designed website can do for your company.

Design transmits your level of professionalism. It brands your business. Companies have doubled their revenue simply by changing their designs, so don't overlook this aspect. Is your website design appealing? Does it reflect your content strategy, and is it user-friendly and easy to navigate, or do you have to click through many pages to find something? Approach your website like a prospect or customer would and think about the experience. How

---

17 Matt Barrie, "How to Make Extra Income from Anywhere," *JamesAltucher.com*, Episode #228, https://jamesaltucher.com/podcast/matt-barrie-how-to-make-extra-income/.

did the site make you feel? Did you find what you were looking for quickly? Is this a site you would visit again?

SEO

Did your web company do its homework on your SEO, your search engine optimization? This will help you rank higher on the organic search engines. Check your SEO yourself. Google your company in incognito browser mode. Search for relevant keywords around your products and services. Does your site appear on the first ranking page, or even on top of the page?

To find out which keywords people are looking for, go to the Google Ads Keyword Planner. There you will find the most popular keywords and the strength of competition around these keywords.

Employ online tools to analyze your current SEO status and show you where the potential lies. You don't have to be a programmer to identify the potential for your website. The site seorch.eu gives you an overview of your website's most important SEO ranking factors. If you see a lot of red, you had better get in touch with a good web development agency to fix it or coach your web development team. Before you hire an agency, check their references and also check their website's SEO ranking.

BUDGET

Your budget impacts your video marketing plan. Some companies produce videos for social media that only run for a month or less. They may be related to a specific event, or they're time-sensitive because of a trend or something going on in the world that makes them time-sensitive. When that's the case, it may not make sense to put all your video budget into this production, unless that is your single most important goal to reach that year. But I would doubt that's the case, right?

Any video production takes effort, and there are different levels of effort. You can produce a good video for a few thousand dollars or spend hundreds of thousands of dollars. Your budget depends on resources and goals. How much do you have to invest in the project for production, where and how long does it need to be distributed to achieve your goal, and what are your quality standards?

Strong channels will help you toward your distribution efforts. You might have a lot of traffic to your website, or followers on your YouTube channel. This gives you a good base for video marketing.

The strength of your channels, along with your goals, also affects how many videos you produce, how often you produce new ones, and how often you run them on paid sites.

Now that you've taken inventory of your current status and have a solid idea of what to do next to get ready for video marketing, let's talk about your potential with video. What can you achieve with video and how will you make it happen? So many opportunities await! Let's explore them all so we can begin to strategize what's best for your business needs, and the needs of your customer.

PRINCIPLES

1. Position yourself—what do you do, and for whom do you do it?
2. Define a basic content strategy, including a style guide.
3. Your most important channel is your website. It's where you convert visitors to customers.

TIPS

1. Ask your customers why they chose you—or did not choose you. Understanding your customer decision is crucial. It's not always about your positioning or your product or service. In many cases it's a combination of reasons. My company receives a lot of positive feedback by responding quickly to email requests. Find out how you stand out! Then make sure you keep doing what they like and fix whatever you're doing wrong.

2. Use online tools to improve your website's performance.
3. Continuously improve your corporate design for your website, videos, photos, graphics, and all visual assets. Professional design transmits trust.

CHAPTER 3

REALIZE YOUR POTENTIAL

A prospective client came to me recently with a nine-page manual describing her brand-new video marketing plan. It was very well structured and thought-through, or so it seemed. She and her team had obviously spent a lot of time developing it, and they were very clear about the company's goals and how they wanted to achieve them. One area of focus was to build up the company's YouTube channel to attract their target group. They wanted to do just four videos a year. The business had no current YouTube followers but thought that by simply posting a video every three months, they could build an audience.

My team and I presented our concern: it would be close to impossible to achieve success with their strategy. Aside from the challenge of building an audience with so few videos, they hadn't clearly defined their target groups. It wasn't clear who they wanted to talk to with their content.

After these prospects pitched some other video production companies for their business, they got back to us. They said they wanted to start over with a clearly defined content strategy before developing their video strategy. The point is, by trying to skip this step, they had wasted a lot of time. If they had done their homework with the content strategy to begin with, we could have been in production by then.

Let's look at another prospect of mine who was so excited about video that he wanted to invest a big part of his marketing budget to produce a single video. After analyzing his current website traffic, I discovered it would not be appropriate for him to invest so much in video only. It made more sense for him to invest in his most important channel first, his website. Optimizing his site would start generating traffic and help him build an audience not only for the site's current content but for any videos he produced and posted there in the future.

These customers didn't have a viable strategy for reaching specific targets, delivering a message, connecting with their customers, or developing an audience. I could have just gone ahead and did what they asked, but I didn't, knowing that when they measured the results, they'd be very disappointed.

Many marketers know marketing very well or at least

have a basic understanding of content strategy, but they don't understand how video works. They struggle to make decisions around their video and social media because the field requires an area of expertise many marketers haven't had a chance to learn yet. It's still a relatively new field that's always changing, and unless a marketer has been actively educating themselves, they get left behind.

This is where going back to the basics I described in chapter 2 really helps. Before you create a nine-page plan on what you want to do with video marketing, take inventory of what you have. See if you have done your homework and defined your target audience and your UVP, and that you have a content strategy ready and a website that drives traffic to it. Survey your entire situation and figure out your potential.

THE VIDEO CUSTOMER JOURNEY

I'm going to tell you about something you've probably never heard of. It's one of my most powerful secrets to video marketing success: the *video customer journey*.

To realize your potential in video marketing, it is crucial to understand that your customers or, better, *potential* customers are on a journey. You have to imagine that everybody is on a different journey and at a different stage. They may be at the beginning (First Point of Contact), in between (Interested, Engaged, Considering) or close to the end of the journey (Convert), when they decide to buy from you.

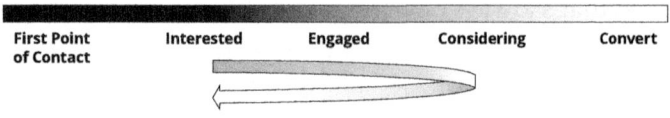

Every Prospect and Customer Is on a Journey from the First Point of Contact with Your Business to Making a Decision or a Deal

Just about anyone with access to video has the potential to become your customer *if* you know who they are, how to reach them, and exactly where they are in their buying decision. That's why it's important to understand the customer journey: so you can align your video marketing accordingly, delivering the right message to the right people, depending on where they are on that journey. Targeting people this way makes the most of your time and your video marketing dollars.

Find your highest converting pages, then see what adding a video or two will do to them. The point is, your customer's journey can be enhanced at some point. You just have to spend some time finding the right point for your business.[18]

Some people have never heard of your company, products, or services. Of course, this is the biggest group and the hardest to capture. You gain their attention either by specific targeted ads or by showing up in their organic search results. You can also capture this audience by word-of-mouth. In any case, they are still in the very beginning of the journey and will advance once they get interested in you.

Others are already engaged with you and are beginning to trust you. In the middle of the journey, people typically engage with you, possibly in different ways. They scan your website because they found you over the internet or they type in your web address from your business card. If you're lucky, the prospect subscribes to your newsletter or even gives you a call to learn more about you.

Still other people are at the brink of making a buying decision, but they need to know what other people who have purchased from you think. Or they need to know more

---

[18] Anna Ji, "Four Myths Stopping Your Business from Producing Great Videos," *Entrepreneur.com*, May 21, 2019, https://www.entrepreneur.com/article/334048.

about your product, like how it works, how much it costs, and if it's going to do what they need it to do.

By this point on the journey, people are considering buying from you. They are comparing different offers from other providers, too. They check the details about your offer. They start imagining how it will be to work with you, when you offer services. Also in this stage the trust factor comes strongly into play. Can I trust this company? Does it have some results to prove? Here is when people turn into paying customers, after a short or long journey.

That's what we call the customer's journey.

The principle of the customer's journey matches one-to-one with the principle of cold, warm, and hot traffic, which some marketers might be familiar with. People at the beginning of the journey are considered cold traffic, in the middle they become warm, and just before they hit the buy button, they are hot traffic. It's very important to distinguish the different forms of traffic since you have to address them differently. This makes your video marketing efforts much more efficient, saving you the cost of targeting the wrong audience with the wrong video.

Before we get into the details of a person's specific location on the customer journey, let's go over some customer basics: cold, warm, and hot traffic.

COLD VS. WARM VS. HOT TRAFFIC

Not every person is a prospective customer, especially if they haven't heard of you or aren't in the market for what you have to offer. Your video marketing strategy should consider whether you're going after that "cold traffic" or the "warm traffic" and how your target market affects the budget. For example, going after cold traffic means casting a wider net on more channels, which can cost more. The target group you go after also affects the results, so you'll want to temper your expectations accordingly.

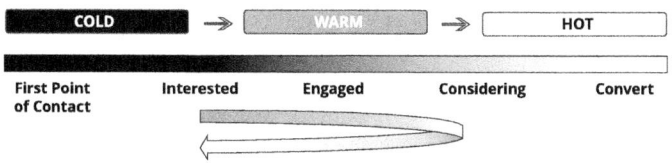

The Stages of a Person's Customer Journey Can Range from Cold to Warm to Hot Traffic

COLD TRAFFIC

The bottom left corner of the bar represents cold traffic, which are people who have never heard of you. You want to give these people the opportunity to connect with you, and you can do that through social media ads, YouTube ads, and TV spots.

Cold traffic includes everybody that is unaware of your

product who might turn into a customer. Watch out; they don't have much time for you. Many marketers make a crucial mistake here: they present a three-minute video and expect people to watch it. In this case, the engagement will be low and so will the results. Cold traffic doesn't trust you yet. It will take time. Cold traffic loves when your video is high quality and you are precise and clear with your message. Imagine how much money is lost in the advertising industry by just transmitting unclear messages—probably billions!

Characteristics of Cold Traffic
- Unaware of your product
- Short attention span for what you have to say
- They don't trust you

How to Get Their Attention
- Be precise
- Be clear
- Transmit your message as quickly as possible

What Turns Them Off
- Poor quality of your video
- Lack of clarity
- Long videos

WARM TRAFFIC

As people become aware of you, they move to the right along the bar in their customer journey, becoming "warm traffic." Now they're interested and engaged and may be considering whether to work with you or buy something from you. They have a demand for your product or service or they expect to need it in the future. You want people who are at this point to see an introduction, image, or brand video of your company. This tells them more about who you are. You position yourself in an exciting way in the video, which appeals to them and draws them in. Positioning, remember, means that you tell them what you do and whom you do it for. You also introduce the UVP or *unique value proposition*, which separates you from the competition. In this image video, which should appear prominently on your website, you show your warm traffic people the value that you provide. This image video needs to be on the first page of your site so people won't miss it or have to search for it. Having it there will also increase the length of time people spend on your site, which in turn improves your ranking on search engines.

Congratulations on your warm traffic. Nowadays in our noisy world with a vast number of globally connected competitors, it is not easy to turn somebody into warm traffic. These potential customers are aware of your solution and are ready to engage with you. They have more time, so the video you address to them can be a bit longer. But please make it as short as possible; don't risk losing them. They love to learn and get smarter around the solution because they have a problem to solve and you might help. Prove it to them with authentic messages. Help them with clear offers. Explain how your product is the best.

As the person becomes engaged, they will be open to learning more about you. An interview or video blog with someone from your company—from the CEO to management and employees—teaches your audience about the culture of the business. Through these types of videos, they get a feel for the values and the mission of the company. If your product is complex, an explainer video may be used to give the audience a short overview of how your product works. Depending on the size of your company, your industry, and your target customers, you might want to do a corporate video at this point.

Characteristics of Warm Traffic

- Aware of your product
- Ready to engage with you
- They want to learn about you

How to Get Their Attention

- Engage with them, show value

- Help them with precise offers and solutions
- Explain how your products work

What Turns Them Off

- Lack of authenticity
- Unclear offers
- Lack of engagement

HOT TRAFFIC

Hot traffic is hot because these people are ready to push the buy button (just kidding—but sometimes they are!). So imagine that these prospects really are all set to buy. The risk of jumping to a competitor's solution might be high. Give them extra trust by presenting a customer's testimonial or show with a product video all the advantages of your product or solution. Tell them what to do next. Add scarcity to your offer (limited supply of product or limited time offer), and your contact might turn into a customer sooner.

Once the person is considering your product, they will have questions and want to know more. This is the perfect place for a product video, which provides a lot more details than the explainer video, or a case study, where you show them how your product solved a problem, provided a solution, or improved a situation for a current customer.

Similarly, testimonials and customer success stories work well when your audience is nearing their decision. They may be comparing you with competitors, and this is where you can show them why you're superior for their needs with a testimonial or success story. The main difference between the two is that a testimonial is typically shorter and less in-depth—an interview of a minute or less. Customer success stories tend to give more details and are a bit longer.

Characteristics of Hot Traffic

- Almost ready to buy
- Risk of changing their mind
- Very aware of your product

How to Get Their Attention

- Show them a customer testimonial or product video
- Tell them what to do next
- Add scarcity

What Turns Them Off

- Complicated sales process
- Long boring messages
- Bad reviews

Now let's translate the customer journey into a *video customer journey*. I designed a solution that helps evaluate the right video for the right time in the journey. It's structured so you can compare different budgets, too, which of course is only vaguely reliable, since so many aspects make up the final costs of a video. Also added is the cycle of the journey after a customer has bought from you. Since existing customers are much more likely to buy from you again, it is important that you pay attention to this group.

The horizontal bar along the bottom of the image, *The Video Customer Journey: A Video for Every Stage of the Customer Journey*, tracks customers on their journey. The vertical bar on the left side of the figure depicts the type of video marketing that's most effective along each phase of the journey, and the size of the budget required.

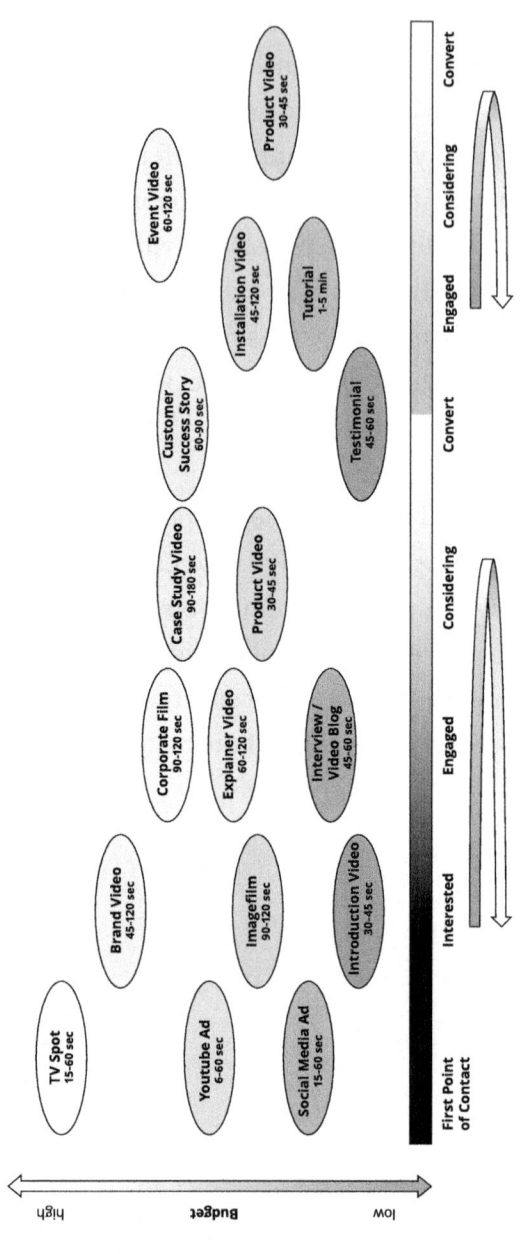

The Video Customer Journey: A Video for Every Stage of the Customer Journey

BREAKING DOWN ALL THE OPTIONS

With so many channels available and groups of people to reach at different stages on the customer journey, deciding where to start can be confusing. Let's talk about your options in detail—what they are, who to reach with them, and what they can do for you.

These are recommendations, and you don't have to follow them strictly. Even though a testimonial is often used to help people make a decision, it can also get the attention of someone who's never heard of you.

What's important here is understanding what the different types of videos are and what they do so you can use them however it makes sense for your industry, company, and target audience.

FIRST POINT OF CONTACT

People at the start of the customer journey aren't aware of you and may not even be looking for what you offer. To develop this market and drive them to your website, you can buy a TV spot, but that can be quite expensive, and you may be paying to reach a lot of people who aren't in your target market. A more cost-effective approach is to target a group and make them aware of your solution with paid video ads on YouTube or social media.

Social Media Ads

Like YouTube ads, social media ads also allow you to engage with a new, likely interested audience. Use these ads to drive that traffic to your website and attract newsletter subscribers.

Short video clips on Facebook, Instagram, and LinkedIn can be targeted toward a specific group and paid for by pay per click. It's easy to measure their results, and some channels, like Facebook, allow you to use A/B testing where you target the same group with two versions of a video, or target two different demographic or geographic groups with one video, and then compare the results.

YouTube Ads

Paid YouTube ads help you engage with a new audience that has a higher than average likelihood of being interested in your product, due to your ability to place them within videos that your market is already watching. For example, if you want to push your new TV show about automobiles, look for popular channels on YouTube about automobiles. There are a lot of channels about automobiles, so it helps if you can get even more targeted, finding one that caters to people who like a specific type of auto. Define your market and your personas as closely as you can and then select the channel that's the best fit to place your ad in.

YouTube is the second largest search engine in the world, offering at least six different ad formats. You can place YouTube ads at the beginning, middle, or end of a video and make them skippable or non-skippable. You can set them up so you pay by the click or have them placed alongside the featured video.

Create an ad that brands your company and drives people to your website. Make sure there's an emotional aspect to it—remember, this is a new audience, and you need to connect with them quickly.

The benefits of using YouTube ads are that they make it easy to target your markets and measure the results. They take many different ad formats and are on the perfect channel for engaging video enthusiasts who spend a lot of time on platforms like YouTube.

The challenges are that this type of video marketing requires resources for distribution and measuring, so you may have to hire an in-house video placement person or a third-party vendor to help you with that piece.

Television Spots

TV spots (commercials, infomercials, etc.) can be used to reach a very large audience. You can purchase local, regional, national, and international ads on broadcast and cable television. TV spots are typically fifteen, thirty, or sixty seconds long, though this has been changing, and some stations are offering spots as short as six seconds. If you decide to go this route, be sure to brand your business with it and include a call to action.

While TV spots have their advantages, it's difficult to target any one group with them, and the results can be hard to measure. Production and placement can be expensive, especially if there are buyout fees. Also known as "right of use," "royalty," "residual," and "usage" fees, buyout fees are paid to actors or voice-over actors for the use of their recorded talent for specific media and for a specified length of time.

INTERESTED IN YOU

At this stage in their customer journey, people are interested in your company, your products, or your services. They are ready to invest more time on your channel. Now is the time to give them the chance to get to know you better. It's not so much about getting their attention at this point—it's about building trust.

Introduction Video

Creating an initial connection with prospective customers can be accomplished with an introduction video. This type of video should aim to build trust between you and your audience.

An introduction video is a simple video where you or your staff introduce yourselves within thirty to forty-five seconds. People love to visit the team site on a website and explore the people they are dealing with, so this is the perfect place for your introduction video. It also can be shared by email with a link to your YouTube channel. While easy to produce, someone from your company will have to get in front of the camera to provide the authenticity required. If they're not used to public speaking, this could be a challenge and require practice—which will be worth the effort.

Image Film

A typical image film focuses first on emotional storytelling. The product or service itself stays mostly out of focus or plays just a subtle role.

The story could explain in an authentic way why the company exists and what value it delivers. If it is a family run business with a long history, then there are certainly many moving and authentic stories to tell. Or it could take the audience on a journey with a customer whose life has changed through the value that the company delivers. Successful image films connect the audience with the story and its protagonists.

Brand Video

A brand video establishes what your company stands for and positions your products and services. It should be authentic and memorable, and you will want to be crystal clear on who you are as a company, your market, and your positioning before you create it. The image you put forth in a brand video can be a deciding factor as to whether people want to do business with you.

Done right, the "branding effect," as it's known, can help establish a loyal customer following. People who connect with a brand are often willing to pay more for a product, and buy additional products, associated with that brand.

Brand videos can be used on your website or in paid ads and also as TV spots. Because brand videos basically show your audience who you are, high-quality production is critical and can be expensive.

ENGAGED PROSPECT

An engaged prospect is a fan of your business. This person is a follower who is eager to learn more about what you have to offer, and they are all ears when you have something to say. Cultivate the engaged prospect with valuable content like interviews and video blogs. Offer them an explainer video to help them understand your new solutions, or a corporate video that provides insights about your company. An engaged prospect will look to you if they need a product that does what yours does, and they will often choose your product over the competition. Video content is a great way to nurture your engaged prospects. In time, they can become loyal brand ambassadors.

Interview/Video Blog

When you have something new to share such as a new product or service, a store opening, a new partnership, or anything else that a person who's already interested in your business will want to know about, try using a video blog or an interview.

Video blogs can be delivered by one person, or they can involve two or more people, interview-style. They come across as authentic, and because they're so easy to produce, you can spread your news quickly and with little production time or cost.

Ideal placement for video blogs is on your website, in your newsletter, and on your social media channel. Depending on the placement, the effect may be short-lived, but sometimes that's all you need to achieve your goal.

Explainer Video

When you have complex descriptions or explanations about your product or service and want to share them in a short amount of time, consider an explainer video. Explainer videos are specifically designed to show how something works—the narrator or actor explains it, and sometimes demonstrates it, in an easy-to-learn format. Since people have different learning styles, explainer videos let you integrate audio, video, text, images, and diagrams to teach people of all types of learning styles how to do something. This video genre is typically animated, but of course there are cross-versions that feature real people.

An important point to remember with explainer videos is to be aware of how you actually show your product. Say your product is being displayed in a person's hand. Are the fingernails clean and trimmed? Because those details affect how the viewer perceives the product in that hand. You may not notice things like this on a small screen, but they will jump out at your customer on a fifty-five-inch 4K TV screen. The focus should be on the product, so be wary of any distractions that can creep into your videos—like a hangnail.

Explainer videos should be engaging and simple to follow. Put them on your website and make them easy to locate. Don't try to make them too long—people will only watch them long enough to find what they need, and these types of videos can be expensive to produce.

Corporate Film

A corporate film focuses on corporate communication and messaging. It is used to engage with specific stakeholders who already know the company. It may be used internally for employee training or externally for promotional intentions around new product lines or services.

The term "corporate film" is broad, encompassing videos used for several purposes. Many corporate films do not have an advertisement character, yet they are still hosted online, usually on a company's About Us page. A person would have to be interested enough in your business to look for it. Still, the corporate film plays an important part on the customer journey.

A corporate film is more of a deep dive into your business than any other video. It shows your audience what you do and how you do it, and may get into the details of each department's people and the processes they follow. The video tells your company story, which may be interesting to you but not always so engaging for other people.

If you opt to create a corporate video, put some serious effort into the preproduction and make sure your story has an emotional component that makes people want to watch it. Get your people involved in the production, too, to ensure a sense of authenticity and a personal connection with viewers.

Corporate videos are typically used only on your website, so their distribution is very limited. However, they can quickly establish a connection with an audience that has actively sought you out and can also boost your SEO, so don't overlook their importance.

CONSIDERING YOU

People who are considering you need to justify their purchase. They are comparing your product with the competitor's, and they want to feel secure in their decision. They might be evaluating the most important features to decide if yours delivers on quality, functionality, warranty, or pricing—whatever is most important to them about the product. A powerful case study or a product video will help convince a prospect who is considering that choosing your product is the right decision.

Product Video

Product videos are useful for removing any doubts a prospect has about your products or services so they can confidently move forward with a purchase. The focus should be on the product's quality and functionality so there are no questions about whether it's the right choice.

Place product videos on your website where people can find them. Though they typically focus on just one product, these videos are short and less costly to produce than most other types of videos and get the job done. They help people who are on the fence about their decision quickly make up their mind.

Case Study Video

Prospects who want to buy from you but are still feeling insecure in their decision can benefit from a case study. This is how you show them proof that your product or service does what you say it does, with facts and real-world examples.

Case studies can be very effective for helping prospects on the verge of a purchase make that final decision. They can be time-consuming to create, so expect a longer than usual production time.

CONVERT PHASE

The break shown about two-thirds of the way across the horizontal line and labeled "Convert" is where your prospect makes a purchase. They are then a customer, represented by the remaining one-third of the line.

This person is very close to deciding whether or not to buy from you—*conversion*. Eliminate any doubt in their mind with a product video that answers all their questions. Or use a customer testimonial or customer success story. These videos are strong emotional mediums that also transmit social proof and can be very effective at this stage of the journey.

Testimonial

A testimonial video establishes credibility for your business by having one of your customers tell about their own experiences with you and your product or service.

Distribution of testimonial videos is typically limited to your website, but they can be produced quickly and easily as long as you have a customer willing to speak on camera. Work with your production team to facilitate the shoot for your "talent"—the customer.

Customer Success Story

Like a testimonial, a customer success story relies on your customer to tell their story. Similar to word-of-mouth advertising, this video is emotion oriented and shows proof of how your product or service works for the customer. Also like the testimonial, a customer success video can be placed on your website. You can also add it to your newsletter.

Customer success stories transmit emotion to customers, increasing the bond you've built with them. They also show real-world examples that your product works for other customers. You will need to find a customer willing to dedicate some time to telling their story, and you'll want to get your video team involved to assist and make it easy for the customer to tell their story.

DON'T FORGET YOUR EXISTING CUSTOMERS

The customer journey doesn't end with a purchase—it goes on. Customers that have once bought from you and are happy with your product or service trust you. They are much more likely to buy from you than from the competition when they need something you both offer.

A customer who is considering buying from you again is very valuable because, most likely, they will. Pay special attention to your existing customers and deliver value with video beyond their first purchase. Answer all their last questions so they can move forward with their purchase. Treat this customer like an ambassador of your brand. Reward them, for example, by inviting them to an event.

According to Marketing Metrics, when selling to a new prospect there is a 5 to 20 percent chance of making the sale. When selling to an existing customer, that probability skyrockets to 60 to 70 percent. Focusing on existing customers makes it easier to sell and grow the business.[19]

Many businesses forget all about marketing once their target has purchased from them. This is a missed opportunity to strengthen the relationship they've worked to develop, and to influence their customers to continue buying more of their product or look at purchasing something else from them.

Tutorial and installation videos show people how to use your product and will improve their success and satisfaction. Your current customers trust you, and they are your best future customers. Don't squander their trust in you or underestimate their future buying power. Continue to invest in these customers with video marketing.

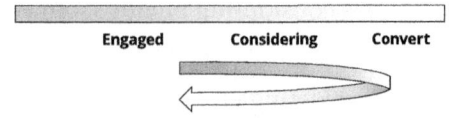

Existing Customers on the Customer Journey

---

19 Joey Coleman, *Never Lose a Customer Again: Turn Any Sale Into Lifelong Loyalty in 100 Days* (New York: Penguin) Kindle Edition, 29.

The curved arrow below the final third of the graph depicts customers who have made a decision or a purchase. This includes purchasing from you or from someone else or deciding not to make a purchase. Once a customer has reached this stage, market to them as Engaged Customers.

An engaged customer is in the process of using your services. What a great opportunity to deliver even more value! You can nurture the relationship and, in many cases, you can lower your customer support efforts.

Because of the targeting capabilities unique to video marketing, a company can closely match its videos to its audience along their journey.

When you're brainstorming your video marketing strategy, focus on emotion-driven content to reach people early in the customer journey. A person will typically be drawn in by content that sparks an emotional response in them when they don't know your company or your product. As they progress in their customer journey, deliver content that's more rational and fact-based.

Installation Video or Tutorial

Prospects want to know that if they buy something from you, they will be able to use it. Your product may require installation or instructions, and this is where an installation video or tutorial comes in handy. A short, simple video that guides customers through the process allays their worries and helps ensure a smooth introduction to the new purchase they're considering.

Distribution of these types of videos is generally limited to the support page of your website. You can also place them on your YouTube channel and email the link to customers.

Quality is not necessarily of the highest importance when it comes to tutorials. They just need to be accurate and easy to follow, and once a customer buys your product, they will lighten the load for your support team.

Event Video

Events like grand openings, new product launches, open houses, trade shows, and sales provide a low-pressure way to engage with prospects who are interested in making a purchase. Promote your event with video from footage at previous events and use new video to wrap up the event and attract people to upcoming events.

Like tutorials, event videos can be placed on your website and YouTube, and you can email the link or put it in your customer newsletter. These videos can bring in a bigger audience to your next special occasion, and if you link them with your lead management, you can continue the conversation with prospects after the event.

Event videos, while a lot of fun to create, can be expensive to shoot and produce. Take time to get the preproduction right so the shoot goes as smoothly as possible—your customers will be watching.

Product Video

Any last doubts a prospective customer has about becoming your customer can be removed with a good product video. They want to know they are about to buy something that's high quality, works the way they need it to work, and solves their problem. Focus on functionality and quality in your product videos.

Product videos should go on your website so people can find them easily. Though they only focus on one product, they are concise and informational and let people know they are buying the right product.

SO WHY DO I NEED SOCIAL MEDIA AND YOUTUBE?

Your customer-facing website is your primary channel and is where you ultimately want to drive traffic. Great content, an attractive and user-friendly design, and SEO will drive people to your site, but you can also use social media and YouTube to get them there.

Like all other channels, social media and YouTube have unique benefits and challenges.

SOCIAL MEDIA

Social media has a short lifespan compared to your company website. You can post a video and get a lot of likes, views, and shares over a few hours' or days' time, but the drop-off in interest is typically dramatic. A week later, no one is looking at it anymore.

If you're serious about using social media within your video marketing strategy, plan on doing it often—daily if possible. The content has to be high quality, too, so if you have a small marketing team, they may not be able to get to it often enough to make it effective. If you can't afford the time or money to make this happen, it may not be a good use of your resources.

YOUTUBE

YouTube differs from traditional social media because it takes many forms, carries different messages, and is used to reach various goals. You can engage video SEO right away to drive people to your videos and get more mileage out of them years later. By simply applying best practices, which I will talk about in more detail, you can reach different goals with YouTube.

- YouTube is unique in that you can place your videos on your channel and then embed them onto your website. In that way, you're showcasing them on your page while simultaneously getting clicks on your YouTube channel, enhancing its rank.
- YouTube videos can also be shared on all your social media channels and embedded into your emails and newsletters. You can allow and encourage people to comment on them and share them with their own friends and followers.
- Use your YouTube videos to engage with people, provide value, and build followers by encouraging them to subscribe to your channel.
- You can also pay to have videos appear on other individuals' or companies' channels (paid media). This takes advantage of audiences that have already been developed and nurtured by others and introduces these people to your company.

THE POWER OF VIDEO

People who have never used video marketing, or who have used it sparingly, may not be aware of its potential.

The power of video is both broad and deep because it can do so many things and do them in a way that isn't possible—or is very difficult—with other media.

- Video allows you to transmit trust and engage with your audience so they want to get to know you more. It shows people what you do and for whom you do it. You can also show your products in use to let people see for themselves that they are attractive, functional, and high-quality.
- Video can be used as a branding tool to display the colors, movement, light, sound, and talent that represent who you are as a company. Showing people a well-produced, high-quality video infers that your products are high quality too.
- Video invokes emotion—a smile, a laugh, a moment of excitement, reflection, contemplation, or enlightenment. People can learn something valuable by watching your video or just come away feeling good. They then associate that feeling with you.
- Video can be a call to action that gets people to try something new. You can invite people to call you, email you, visit your website or store, subscribe to your newsletter, follow and communicate with you on YouTube and social media, and—of course—place an order with you. All of these can be accomplished in a one-minute video.
- Video can tell a story that connects with a person's

emotions and is memorable. Your audience may not remember all the facts they read about a product, but if you put the content into a story they can relate to, they will be more likely to recall it.
- Videos help you address customers' common questions and problems and cut down on support calls. Installation videos and tutorials show customers how to use and troubleshoot a product without making a phone call or sending an email, and they have access to these videos any time of the day or night. Fast access to this kind of support can also prevent bad reviews.
- Video marketing on your website, social media, and YouTube can be measured more granularly, and you can adjust your marketing based on those measurements more quickly than any other media. This empowers you to continuously improve your marketing.

GETTING STARTED: QUESTIONS TO ASK YOURSELF BEFORE YOU DEVELOP YOUR VIDEO MARKETING STRATEGY

Like any marketing effort, before you jump into video marketing you should figure out what you want to accomplish and how you're going to do it. Ask yourself these questions and take some time to answer them. Rushing into video marketing without clearly identifying your resources, goals, and audience can be costly and ineffective.

- What is your goal? What are you trying to make happen with video marketing?
- Who needs to see your videos for you to accomplish that goal? This is your target audience.
- What is your message? Focus on your unique value proposition (UVP). What value do you deliver, how do you deliver it, and what differentiates you from competitors?
- What channels will you use to reach viewers? This depends on your target audience and where you are most likely to find them, so you need to know what channels they are already watching.
- What types of videos do you want to make? What types can you afford to make and distribute?

We'll talk about all of these factors in the next chapter.

PRINCIPLES
1. Every type of video has a place and a goal on the customer's journey.
2. Start with your website and expand from there with a multichannel strategy.
3. Don't underestimate who you can reach and what you can transmit with just one minute of video.

TIPS

1. If you are undecided about the message to transmit with video, focus on the value you can provide to your customers with tutorials and explainer videos.
2. Don't forget your existing customers. These people already trust you.
3. Use people in your videos to make them more engaging.
4. Don't forget to include a call to action in your video.

CHAPTER 4

STRATEGIES FOR IMPLEMENTING VIDEO

As a marketer, you have goals to reach and a limited budget with which to accomplish them. You align your goals to your budget and use all your resources wisely so you don't go over budget or run out of money. It's the same with your video marketing implementation: you need a strategy that takes into account what you need to get done *and* how much money you have to do it.

Before you go into production, figure out what you want to achieve and devise an affordable and realistic strategy to make it happen. In addition to goals and budget, consider factors like your time frame, weaknesses or issues in your current marketing strategy or business situation, and immediate problems that need to be solved. Your particular industry and your market, and the current situations of each, could even play a part in choosing the best strategy.

I've outlined four basic strategies for you to consider: Single Video Strategy, Customer Journey Strategy, Campaign Strategy, and Cultivation Strategy. In my experience, these cover just about everything a marketer has asked me to help them accomplish. Keep in mind that you can't make miracles happen with a tiny budget. Likewise, if you have a good-sized budget and only a few minor goals, do some exploring and see what else you can achieve. You could be thinking too big—or too small.

Your video implementation strategy includes a distribution strategy—the channels and methods you use to get your video in front of your customers—which should be included within the budget. Depending on your implementation strategy, number of videos, quality of production, and distribution strategy, the distribution budget could be very low—such as one where you only place a few videos on your website—to many times the production cost, such as for a worldwide distribution with international TV spots. In chapter 9, which discusses distribution strategies, we'll talk about that part of your implementation in greater detail.

SINGLE VIDEO STRATEGY

The single video strategy is a good choice for companies that haven't started using video yet, have a limited budget, and want the greatest results for a low investment.

SINGLE VIDEO STRATEGY: THE "QUICK FIX STRATEGY"

If you have an issue that needs a quick fix, the single video strategy is the way to go. You could have a product that needs some explaining, and you're getting a lot of support calls. An installation or tutorial video solves that problem. Or your business has a sudden image issue. An authentic video that reassures customers that you're aware of the problem, care about how it's affecting people, and are actively fixing it may be the first video you need to make.

If you don't have a specific problem to fix, then begin with an image video or a testimonial. A sixty- to ninety-second video on your landing page quickly positions your company while communicating your unique value proposition and your company's values. Make it authentic and emotion-based to build trust. A video of facts and figures where you talk only about yourself will not engage customers, so always remember that it is about them. Tell them how you bring them value. Alternatively, produce a testimonial video with one of your satisfied customers. Either way, the production and channel costs for these videos are very low. You post your single video only on your most important channel, your website, so you don't have to pay anyone for distribution.

BEFORE YOU CHOOSE THE SINGLE VIDEO STRATEGY

While this strategy is efficient, effective, and maintenance free—you simply "set it and forget it"—it only addresses one stage in the customer journey. Still, if you have a limited budget and a simple goal, the single video strategy is the best way to go.

SINGLE VIDEO STRATEGY: THE QUICK FIX STRATEGY

When Is This Strategy Right for You?

- You have a small budget
- You are just starting off with video marketing
- You expect the best results for the money

Best Video Genres for the Single Video Strategy

- Image video
- Testimonial
- Introduction video

Results to Expect When the Single Video Strategy Is Done Right

- Higher conversion rate
- More engagement (visitors stay longer on your website)
- You build trust

Good to Know about the Single Video Strategy

- It only works when you already have a good amount of traffic to your website
- Even if you only have one video, don't try to communicate *everything,* so focus on one message
- A bad video can do more harm than good—stick to quality

CUSTOMER JOURNEY STRATEGY

The customer journey strategy works well for a medium budget where you want to reach prospects and customers at multiple touch points on the journey. Here, you produce several videos specific to your targets at each stage.

The customer journey strategy covers the whole journey your customer goes on. It's the best way to communicate with people on their path to buying from you. On every touch point on the journey, you can answer questions through videos, gain trust, engage, and convert. Of course, you need a budget that allows for strategic planning from preproduction through post-production. It is definitely my favorite strategy, especially for people who want to cover a lot of ground in one production.

CUSTOMER JOURNEY STRATEGY: THE "SUSTAINABLE STRATEGY"

The customer journey strategy is sustainable because it moves people through all the stages, from having never heard of you to becoming a repeat customer. Start by exploring your current situation and decide where you have the biggest problems that need to be addressed, or the greatest opportunities that you can capitalize on by reaching target groups at specific stages.

If you aren't attracting enough new business, maybe you should start at the beginning of the journey with paid YouTube ads embedded into your website. If prospects seem to stay engaged for a while but end up buying from a competitor or not buying at all, look at the decision stage and focus your initial efforts there by putting a testimonial on your product page.

If you're having several videos produced initially, choose three or more stages to focus on, and if you have the budget, consider doing twenty or more videos. You might have an introductory video, an image video, five testimonials, five product videos, five explainer or installation videos, two customer case studies, and an event video. Ultimately, you will want to have at least one video for each stage, so there are no weaknesses in your implementation. This way, you will be engaging with prospects and customers every step of the way.

The main channel for a customer journey strategy is your website. Place the videos where they make sense: an image video on the landing page, tutorials on the support page, testimonials on the product page, and so on.

Producing several videos at the same time is more cost-effective because your production team can do several or all of the shoots at one time instead of scheduling multiple shoots. This means less downtime and fewer interruptions for your business, too. Creating videos in groups helps with consistency and continuity because you will have the same team working on the videos during a specific time frame, all following the same style guide. You'll have a chance to see how all the videos play together, complementing each other and telling a fluid story for the prospect and customer along their journey.

BEFORE YOU CHOOSE THE CUSTOMER JOURNEY STRATEGY

Before you opt for a customer journey strategy, ensure that you have a strong website. It should be built on a current platform and be attractive, well designed, and technically robust and able to handle the traffic.

CUSTOMER JOURNEY STRATEGY: THE SUSTAINABLE STRATEGY

When Is This Strategy Right for You?

- You have enough budget for several videos
- You want to cover the whole journey
- You are thinking very strategically

Best Video Genres for the Customer Journey Strategy

- Image video
- Testimonial
- Product video

Results to Expect When the Customer Journey Strategy Is Done Right

- *Dramatically* higher conversion rate
- Less customer support needed
- Ability to compare the results of different videos

Good to Know about the Customer Journey Strategy

- Invest a good amount of time in investigating your touch points with your customers
- Try to produce as many videos as you can in one batch to save time and money
- Compare the performance of each video and take action when needed

CAMPAIGN STRATEGY

The fastest way to get your product out there in the public eye is with a campaign strategy. Though costlier than the previous strategies, a campaign strategy quickly brands your business and drives people to your website. If you want to attract attention fast, or you need to spread the news about an event, product launch, or relaunch and you have enough money in your budget, this is the strategy for you.

If you have very specific goals to reach fast and the budget for production and for distribution, then the campaign strategy is best. According to your target group, you can go with selected social media channels starting with paid video ads. If you have enough time, don't shy away from A/B testing. This will help to make your campaign more effective. Compare different versions of your videos and different channels and analyze the results.

CAMPAIGN STRATEGY: THE "FAST RESULTS STRATEGY"

The campaign strategy comprises from one to ten—sometimes more—different videos spread across different paid channels, including YouTube, social media, and TV ads, with the goal of driving traffic to your site and converting prospects to customers. You can use redirects or special URLs so people land on specific pages on your site where they can make a purchase, subscribe to your newsletter, or speak with someone at your company. The advantage of this is easy-to-measure responses, including impressions and clicks, which you can leverage for continuous improvement and better results.

Add split testing by producing several similar videos that target different audiences or promote different products, see which ones get the most conversions, and put your distribution budget behind those. The campaign strategy is perfect for figuring out what works best on the fly and adjusting your budget to optimize results.

Have you ever seen a company come out of nowhere, and suddenly it seems like it's everywhere? This is how a campaign strategy works. Getting your targeted videos on multiple paid channels increases the visibility and sensitizes your audience to them, so they'll be more apt to notice them each time they appear. This is one way to get people to know and remember you. Make your campaign videos exciting or thought-provoking with an emotional tone for the best results.

BEFORE YOU CHOOSE THE CAMPAIGN STRATEGY

Expect your distribution costs for a campaign strategy to make up a higher percentage of your video budget than other strategies. You will be placing paid ads on many channels.

CAMPAIGN STRATEGY: THE FAST RESULTS STRATEGY

When Is This Strategy Right for You?

- You want fast results
- You can afford paid media (such as paid YouTube and social media video ads)
- You want to do A/B testing

Best Video Genres for the Campaign Strategy

- YouTube video ads
- Facebook video ads
- TV spots

Results to Expect When the Campaign Strategy Is Done Right

- Much more traffic to your website
- More specific traffic to your website (due to targeted video ads)
- Continuous improvement due to analytics on your social media ad manager

Good to Know about the Campaign Strategy

- Don't underestimate the distribution budget
- You need time and resources to manage the distribution
- Highly effective for timed campaigns and those demanding fast results

CULTIVATION STRATEGY

Maybe you haven't started using video or you've used it only sporadically, so you haven't built an audience. If this is your goal and you have a substantial, ongoing budget, look to the cultivation strategy.

Build up your audience over time. With time and the weekly resources to produce great content, you can provide great value for your viewers. Remember, in order to pick the fruits from your effort, you have to go a long way.

Most of the successful channels on YouTube produced dozens of videos before they could feel an impact.

CULTIVATION STRATEGY: THE "GROW YOUR AUDIENCE STRATEGY"

The cultivation strategy raises awareness around who you are and establishes your credibility. It's how companies create a loyal fan base. But you need to do it regularly with frequent posts—at the very least, every week—to YouTube and social media.

Using hired talent such as a celebrity, social media influencer, or brand ambassador gives people someone to connect with and "follow" in your cultivation videos. Create ads, add text and create video blogs, and place these on your YouTube channel. Then share them to other sites, such as your webpage and Facebook page. Over time, you will get subscribers and as they comment, like, and share the videos, your audience grows.

BEFORE YOU CHOOSE THE CULTIVATION STRATEGY

Along with requiring a big budget, this strategy is time-consuming, and it also takes time to get results. It requires a dedicated team or at least one full-time person on your staff to ensure videos are produced and posted regularly, and that person will need a backup—or have to have videos made and scheduled ahead of time—if they ever want to take some time off.

The cultivation strategy isn't for every business. Fashion, lifestyle, entertainment, health, and entrepreneurship are industries that typically do well with it. Every niche has a chance to cultivate an audience as long it delivers value. Think about how your product lends itself to this strategy: Do you have something new to show people on a regular basis (and they will buy on a regular basis), like a designer line of clothing, jewelry, or makeup? Do you have a strong product or brand that's visually exciting, and a target that loves digital media? If you have all that and want to grow an audience, this is the way to do it.

Whatever strategy you choose, remember that your customers are always on a journey and it's your job to build trust and deliver value at every step. Think of every video you produce and distribute as a touch point for building and strengthening that trust.

CULTIVATION STRATEGY: THE GROW YOUR AUDIENCE STRATEGY

When Is This Strategy Right for You?

- You are disciplined and patient
- You have the resources to support weekly video marketing (at least once a week)
- You are thinking long term

Best Video Genres for the Cultivation Strategy

- Tutorials
- Product videos
- Interviews

Results to Expect When the Cultivation Strategy Is Done Right

- A gradual and continuous increase in followers
- An engaged community
- You can position yourself as an influencer

Good to Know about the Cultivation Strategy

- Look for role models in your industry first (some formats don't work as well as others)
- You can batch productions to save money
- Consider installing your own studio

TARGETED VIDEO MARKETING

Targeted video marketing focuses on a specific market by running ads where your target groups already are. Someone or something already has this market's attention with their content, and you put your video alongside it or within it. The options are very granular, from putting your ads on a particular YouTube video channel to placing them within a specific video. You can target a demographic—women from eighteen to twenty-five within a specific geography and income range, for example. On LinkedIn, you can target a company instead of individual prospects so you're not spending money attracting unwanted clicks and views that you have to pay for. Videos on YouTube and social media do this better than any other marketing combination. They are easy to measure, and you can get a lot of valuable information about your market and their interests from the results.

A good example of this is a tap-dancing channel, where someone provides free dance lessons to their subscribers. If you sell tap dance shoes or portable tap dance flooring, wouldn't you want to run an ad in that channel? Your prospective buyers are already watching that channel, so you won't have to chase them down. The tap dance instructor already has their attention! Ads like this can be placed at the beginning as a non-skippable six-second bumper ad, or they can be placed as in-stream ads that can be skipped after five seconds. On YouTube, there are a vast number of video ad options to consider.

Behavior-driven placement is also a consideration in targeted marketing. If you analyze traffic to your website and discover most people visit between the hours of 3 and 5 p.m., you can run ads during that time. Maybe a high percentage of people access your website from their phones instead of their desktops between 5 and 7 p.m.; that's another consideration that affects not only when you run videos but the format you use. Of course, the length of your video, where, when, and how often it appears, and all the other options affect your cost.

Targeting your audience is most effective with paid marketing. You can't post videos on your website and always expect the right people to land on your page. It doesn't work that way. But you can target groups of people with paid ads on YouTube and other sites and drive them to your website.

To do targeted video right, you'll need a dedicated resource: someone whose job it is to analyze your distribution options, place your ads, and record the results. They'll have to analyze the responses and use the data to improve your distribution. This can become very complex quickly, so some companies hire an outside vendor that specializes in media placement.

Talk to your video production company about targeted marketing during the preproduction process. They may have someone on staff who can do this for you or coach you, or they might be able to refer you to someone.

YOUR BUDGET: THE ENERGY THAT DRIVES YOUR STRATEGY AND YOUR GOAL

Think of your budget as energy—all the energy you have to put behind your video marketing strategy. You won't be able to start a massive campaign or fulfill a huge distribution plan on a small budget. Sure, anyone can make a video with a smartphone, post it to social media, and call it a campaign, but the point is to achieve some kind of goal. That requires a certain quality and strategy that can't be met without a budget. Goal, budget, and strategy go hand in hand and each one affects the others.

Marketers are familiar with the 80/20 rule, where 80 percent of your results come from 20 percent of your efforts. Think of your video marketing the same way, especially if your budget is limited. What kind of video strategy will give you the most bang for your buck?

With a big budget, you can play around a little—experiment, measure, and improve. But if your budget is small, you don't have that luxury. You'll want to do your homework and really think about how to get the most from your investment. Examine each stage of the customer journey and discover the precise stage where video is likely to have the greatest impact toward your goal.

If you have the budget for it, you can combine strategies, too. You might want to start a long-term cultivation plan to build a fan base while running a hard-hitting campaign to introduce a new product. Of course, you'll want to make sure your website is in perfect order before doing either of those so you can support the traffic and make the best possible impression on all your new visitors.

Whatever your budget is, talk to your video professionals. Some full-service production companies can step you through the whole process, or most of it. If they can't, ask them for a referral. However, if you're working with a producer who doesn't understand content marketing and simply follows your instructions, make sure you know exactly what you're doing, hire a pro to guide you, or look for another production company. Optimally, your marketing department's content marketing people and video production people will have a good working relationship so they can collaborate to turn out the best possible productions for your business.

Figuring out your budget starts with looking at how much money you have in your marketing budget and deciding how much of it you want to dedicate to video. Think about how aggressive you want to be. I've had clients spend $10,000 on video production and $2,500 on distribution, and others spend $100,000 on the production and *twice* that—$200,000—on a very aggressive multichannel distribution schedule. So quality and distribution, and how you balance them, are also budget considerations.

The channels you use, how many you use, how many videos you want to produce, and the competition for your product and for your audience are also factors to think about. Testing with multiple campaigns, channels, demographics, geographic locations, A/B tests, and more add to the cost, so think about what you want to accomplish and the best way to get there with your available resources. Again, talk to your video professionals for advice.

If your budget is very limited, start with channels you own, beginning with your website. Believe it or not, your website is the most powerful content channel. Anything you put there can serve you in the long term, unlike TV spots or social media that work well in the short term but have a short shelf life. Your website is also very targeted. Think about it: Who visits your site other than people who already know about you or find you in a Google search?

Get your site in tip-top shape and then start with inexpensive choices, such as introductory and branding videos for the landing page and testimonials for your product pages. Once your website is populated with videos for each stage of the customer journey, look to your next budget to get some paid, short videos that drive people to your site so they can see all the excellent videos you have there. Think about the four video implementation strategies and decide which one is for you, get a quote from your video production team, and get ready for the next step: making videos!

PRINCIPLES

1. Get clear on your goals for your video implementation.
2. Figure out your budget and decide how you will balance production and distribution costs.
3. Choose the right strategy according to your goals and your budget. These three factors—strategy, goal, and budget—must all work together for your video implementation to be a success.
4. Measure your results.

TIPS

1. Think long term—you will always be improving on what you've done before.
2. Don't forget to include the distribution costs in your budget.

3. Plan on producing several videos so you can reach different targets and measure the results of different videos, potentially on different channels and targeting different markets.
4. To establish trust with your audience, have more than one testimonial video on your website and a high-quality image video. The company CEO is a good interview subject for this type of video.

ACT II

LET'S GO INTO PRODUCTION

CHAPTER 5

WHY YOU SHOULD HIRE A VIDEO PRODUCTION COMPANY

Last year around the winter holidays, a prospective client contacted me to produce two testimonial videos for his company. This was his first foray into video marketing, and he wanted the video to go live in early January—giving me roughly three weeks from start to finish.

I didn't say "no," but I knew right away that I would be spending some time up front educating this person about what goes into video production. He would have to get agreement from his customers to perform in the testimonial. My team needed to prepare the right questions in order to get the statements we needed from the client's customer so we could tell a story with the video. A production date hadn't been set, so the different parties needed to find time on the same day for the shoot. We also had to consider the additional time required for post-production, which would involve going back and forth with the client and the client speaking with his customer.

We would have to discuss the strategy, budget, message, audience, and possible distribution channels. After completing preproduction, production, and post-production, we'd need to place the video and begin measuring the results. A good full-service video production company can do all these things, but they need time to do them right.

Educating people about the process is typically one of my first tasks when working with a new client. They're often surprised by the time and resources required to get started. This is understandable, as video marketing is different in many ways from any other type of marketing, and every production has its own dynamic. A few of my customers need the approval of their entire marketing staff about practically everything. Sometimes it takes them several days to get back to us. These numerous inputs require us, the video production company, to be prepared to explain why we made certain decisions. Satisfying everyone affects decisions such as the rhythm of the cuts, the timing, the music, the choice of statements, the voice, and more. Anyone who doesn't commit to the field full-time is not likely to be aware of all the requirements, opportunities, and challenges. This is one reason why, even if you have your own in-house video production department, it might make sense to hire a full-service company to manage your video marketing.

Despite this client's initial expectations, once I stepped him through a process that I knew would deliver a positive outcome, he was on board. He quickly realized that he and his team had a lot of questions to answer first. They also had legal issues to work out around the content. Their website wasn't prepared to host the video, and they hadn't even considered who their target audience was or how they could reach them.

We couldn't launch his video marketing campaign in early January like he wanted, but once he had done all the homework on his end, we went into production in early February and completed all the editing approvals in time to launch his initial video in late March. Thanks to his willingness to put in the time and effort, our collaboration was a tremendous success.

You might wonder why I didn't turn down this client, knowing I couldn't meet his timeline. If I had, he probably would have called another production company. They may have agreed to do the video in four weeks, which meant doing it with no serious workflow or anything else that's required for a successful video launch. I didn't want to see that happen, so I agreed to work with him but I also explained what he should expect, how long it would take, and how much it would cost.

A good rule of thumb is "It always takes longer than you think." When I agree to take on a new client, the timeline is typically delayed by the client and their responsibilities, not by the actual production process. This is because marketers new to video just don't have the big picture they need to get started.

Customers are often surprised by the cost involved, too, and they sometimes try to do the video in-house to save money. They might bring me in as a consultant. One client hired me to step her through the preparation, but then she needed me to help her with all the on-camera work, such as lighting and coaching her talent. Each time a challenge arose, she called me for help. She would eventually need me to do all the post-production work, too, because she did not have enough editing experience. After several sessions, the client realized it would be easier and more cost-effective to simply hire my production company to do the job for her.

YOU CAN'T KNOW EVERYTHING

This client wasn't lacking all the typical knowledge a marketing professional brings to the table. In fact, she knew as much about video marketing as most of the people who hire me. Marketing has become so complex in the past decade that experts tend to specialize—there are content managers, conversion rate specialists, digital communication specialists, and many more roles that didn't even exist in the recent past—and you can't specialize in every single facet. On top of that, digital marketing is changing so fast that no one can be expected to keep up with it unless it's their full-time job. So if you're managing all the marketing for a business, there's no way you're going to be able to keep up with how fast video marketing—production, distribution, social media channels, SEO, and all the rest of it—changes.

Big companies can afford to make a bunch of videos. They have an advantage, with more resources (including AI, artificial intelligence), so they can invest more time and money into measuring customer behavior such as engagement on different channels and different videos. They can also create more reliable reports that guide their future decisions. Instead of making just one video, they can afford to make four videos and use split testing to track, measure, and compare the results. This ability to measure more details of their marketing results faster and respond more quickly to the changes taking place gives them a big advantage over companies that don't have the same resources. As a small- to mid-sized company, it's tough to compete without some outside, expert help.

Did you have coursework in video marketing in college? Or even content management? These are very new additions to marketing curricula, and many colleges still haven't added them. Fortunately, you don't have to do it on your own. You just have to find the right video production company.

WHAT A FULL-SERVICE PRODUCTION COMPANY CAN DO FOR YOU

Video production is complex. A video *itself* is complex—when done right. There are a lot of moving pieces, and if you get one of them wrong, it can bring down the whole production. You need the right story, images, and talent. You need good quality video and audio recording, too. These are things that an experienced producer is aware of and can help ensure that you get right the first time.

A good producer makes sure your story transports a key message that the audience will understand. He ensures the images and words complement each other and that you don't give the viewer a reason to click away from your video before it ends. An audio engineer listens for background noise on a set that you may not even notice: a lawn mower passing under a window, an air conditioner humming in the ceiling, or a jet flying overhead. All those things you're not aware of, the producer has dealt with hundreds of times and is thinking about before, during, and after the shoot.

Marketers come to me after they've tried to do their own videos, or after they've worked with a production company that simply followed directions and did everything the marketer told them to do. The proof of this method is, as they say, in the pudding, and the final results range from bad to horrible. My team and I have seen just about every video disaster you can imagine:

1. No clear message. The video is trying to say *something*—but what?
2. Too many messages. You can only squeeze so much into a short video. Overloading it with multiple messages will bury your most important message at best. At worst, it will totally confuse—and turn off—your viewer.
3. Cognitive overload. Same here: *too much* going on with live action, sound, and images. Knowing how much is *too* much is an important skill in video production. Going overboard doesn't create a memorable impact for your audience but a painful experience that's soon forgotten.
4. No story line. The best videos tell a story and connect with people on an emotional level.

5. Content that isn't relevant nor engaging. Know your target audience and what interests them.
6. Too many words to read. They fill the entire screen, scroll up, or crawl across the video, and there are so many words that fly past or blink off before anyone can read them.
7. Font that's too small for a video that's going to be viewed primarily on a mobile phone, or too large to be comfortably read on a desktop computer or television.
8. Bad lighting, bad acting, and bad audio. These problems are not always correctable in post-production or with a new production team, so we have to start all over again.
9. No authenticity. The narration sounds like a bad marketing script from the 1990s. These videos make me cringe because the company has squandered an opportunity to show their audience who they really are and invite them to join them in their shared values.
10. No call to action. "Wow, that video was great! If only it told me how to contact the company, buy the product, learn more…"

In addition to all the technical issues, a producer can help you with your strategy. He will talk to you about your goals and your budget and tell you the truth about what you should expect to accomplish. He'll encourage you to have a content strategy first and a style guide, so that your videos are consistent and fit well with your other marketing. And he'll give you an honest assessment of your current channels, such as your website and your YouTube channel, instead of taking your money and making you a video that won't do you any good because your channels are all wrong.

A producer will think ahead about your production standard and how your graphics, logos, intros, and outros can be produced and repurposed to save you money on future productions. He also acts as an outside observer, providing objective feedback on your strategy and content.

Hiring a video production company lets you offload all the things you don't know and don't have to know to do your marketing job so you can focus on the details you do know, and those you need to develop, to get a video that represents your company, products, and services, and achieves your goals.

If you have an in-house production department you can still hire a production company and collaborate with them, so you're working together on different parts of the production. Maybe you have a really great camera guy who has done excellent shoots for your business, but you need help with your strategy and distribution. Or maybe you have a studio onsite with all the lighting and soundproofing and a full production team that's capable of producing your videos but isn't up to speed on all the latest improvements in video quality. You can contract a professional producer to coach your team and guide the production, taking advantage of your current resources while enjoying the advantages of having a video pro on the team. Knowing what your strengths and weaknesses are will help you choose the best video coach for your needs.

If you choose to do all the video production yourself, you may still want to hire a professional brand ambassador to represent your company on-camera or use someone in-house who's a good speaker for the job. If you use a nonprofessional actor, such as the CEO of the company, I recommend they get media training first. They should become familiar with being "onstage" and work on their performance in front of the camera. Alternatively, you can partner with known influencers who have their own production teams to come to your site and make a video about your products.

HIRING THE RIGHT COMPANY

There's a book by Thomas J. Elliott called *The Death of the Traditional Video Production Company* that makes the case for reactive video producers at death's door. Elliott proposes that they rather turn into a proactive visual content agency with all the necessary services and solutions to provide real and verifiable value. I agree with this and strongly recommend that in your search for a company to partner with, you find out how much they know about the entire process: from developing video strategies to preproduction through to distribution. They might be able to help you with measuring and analytics too, or at least be able to refer you to an expert for that piece.

TOP 5 QUESTIONS TO ASK BEFORE YOU HIRE A VIDEO PRODUCTION COMPANY

1. Are they goal and target group oriented?

2. Are they good listeners?

3. Where is the focus?

4. What's the offer?

5. What about video and audio quality?

You will build a much stronger relationship with your video producer than you have with the people you work with in other media. If you run print advertising, you might create your own flyer or insert and send it to your representative to get into whatever magazine, newspaper, or mailer they represent. With video, expect to spend some time with the producers and think of them as an extension of your marketing department. They will need to well understand your company, your culture, your products and services, and who you create them for. They should have a very clear plan and ask you about your goals, your message, who you want to reach, and where your target prospects and customers are in their customer journey. You will be putting some time into this relationship, so don't take it lightly or think that if you don't like the first company you hire, you can easily switch to a different one for your next video. Think of your production company as an employee who you are hiring for the long term. Otherwise, you will be re-educating new people every time you want to make a new video.

Look for a company that's local so you can meet with them face-to-face and so they can come to your site for meetings and shoots. Check out their website and look at their production quality. Is their website attractive, engaging, and easy to navigate? Do you want the people who designed it to design your videos and help you with distribution? Look at their testimonials and other videos too so you can get an idea of the types of videos they do and how they appear.

To find a local company, you can do an online search for video production companies in your area or look at the websites of local businesses, find those that include videos, and see which ones you like the most. You might be able to figure out the name of the production team on the website, but if it's not obvious, try calling the business and asking them. Look at the video producer's website and videos. Are they authentic? Do they communicate trust? Is their messaging clear and engaging? What about the audio quality? Watch out; some production companies do very high-end videos, but that's *all* they do. They won't help you with your story, your message, or the distribution because they are used to having all that done by another agency that also brings their own director. Just because someone has a flashy video on their website doesn't mean they'll be able to take care of your specific needs.

Once you find a company that looks like a good fit, meet with them to learn about their process and rates. Don't rely on what their website says—websites tell a lot of stories that don't always reflect the facts about a business. Find out if they know about different strategies and about the customer journey and see if they are knowledgeable enough to assist you with whatever you don't know about video marketing. Spend some time with them and see if you will like working with them. Remember, this will be a long-term relationship, like hiring an employee, so you want to choose the best candidate who is a good fit for your team, can do the job, and can do it within your budget. They may not know everything, and their process and the terminology they use to describe it may be different than mine, but you still must spend some time and make sure they can deliver what you need.

Finally, ask them for a reference—someone the company has worked with that you can contact for an honest opinion on what it's like to work with them. Then you can begin the preproduction process.

QUESTIONS TO ASK WHEN CHOOSING A VIDEO PRODUCTION COMPANY

Put some time and effort into choosing a video company. You may be collaborating with these people on a number of projects over many years. They may even outlast your own employees. Following are detailed questions to ask yourself and prospective video production companies before making this important decision.

LOOK AT THEIR VIDEOS

The best place to start evaluating a video company is by looking at their products—their videos.

Are they goal and target group oriented?

Remember that video marketing has a goal and targets a specific audience. Even if you don't know the exact goal of a video, as a viewer you should be able to get a feel for that goal. Does the content grab you, pull you in a specific direction, speak to you as a possible target, and motivate you to take action? If it does, that producer had a goal and a target group in mind.

Is it an overload?

Most advertisement or video ads nowadays do not consider our short attention spans or our high tendency for distraction. Do the videos you are inspecting address this issue? Is there a clear message with information and emotion that can be absorbed by the audience? If you get bombarded with dozens of facts and feel no emotion, then it's not a match.

What about the story and flow of their videos?

Watch a couple of short videos from the production company from beginning to end. Do you feel any flow and rhythm? Does it take you on an emotional journey? Does it excite you? Does it *move* you?

How is their video quality?

There are many technical aspects to video quality, and too many details for this book. But you should be able to see whether the overall video quality feels right and matches your company's expectations. Do the colors feel right for you? Are the contrasts well defined and the frames carefully chosen? Go with your gut and compare the production company's videos with benchmark videos that you admire.

Is the audio any good?

Pay close attention to the audio! This is often overlooked, yet audio can greatly affect a video's results and success. Listen closely to the sound quality. What about the soundtracks and sound effects? Do the producers use them, and do they enhance the audio experience?

GET TO KNOW THE PEOPLE

Find out who you're going to be dealing with. The best video production company in the world won't make you happy if the people don't care about your goals or are difficult to work with.

Do they listen to you?

Good storytellers (who will be telling your company's story) must also be good listeners. Call them and have a conversation, and meet with them in person if possible. Find out how interested they are in you, your company, and your goals before you commit to them. Ask them questions about their business, too.

Do they seem confident and knowledgeable? Do you like them and feel like you can trust your video marketing to them? Finally, do they seem truly interested in what you want to achieve, or are they pushing you to sign a contract?

Where is the focus?

If their website doesn't make this clear, then ask them. Video production is a wide field, and the more specialized the company is to meet your needs, the better. For example, some production companies specialize in corporate videos, while others are highly skilled in TV production. Still others have a terrific distribution team that understands video placement across all the channels. Find the right fit for your business.

What is *their* why?

Good video producers are good storytellers. What is their own story? Find out why they are doing video in the first place, and you might discover a lot of details about their motivation and engagement not just with the process but also with you.

ASK ABOUT THEIR PRODUCTION PROCESS

By now, you have a good understanding of the production

process. See how the production company's lines up with your expectations.

What does the overall production process look like?

Does the company take time for preproduction and carefully lay out the production details? Or do they want to start shooting right away? A company that pushes you into production could be a costly mistake!

How will we get to a story?

Make sure the company takes the time to speak with you by phone or video conference or in person to carefully develop the story. A good video production company has a plan and structure for doing this. Find out whether they have one. They should ask you a lot of questions and want to know the story of your company, its values, who your customer is, and what you want to achieve with video marketing.

How many turnovers do I get in post-production?

Find out how many revisions are included in the post-production and make sure it's clearly stated in the offer. I typically propose a minimum of two revisions for clients.

How long will the turnover time be?

The overall post-production process depends on the production company, but it's also affected by how quickly you provide them with feedback. Find out what their typical turn-around time for a video is once post-production begins, and if you have a deadline, address that with the company and see if they can meet it.

OTHER QUESTIONS TO ASK

Other questions may not seem important now, but they could become very important down the road.

What is the offer?

That's the first question we usually get asked, and so often, it's misleading. Pricing doesn't tell you anything if you don't take into account the promised outcome. Check their offer carefully and make sure you understand every detail. I repeat, *every detail.* You should understand how much goes into the story creation, how much goes into production, and how much goes into distribution. How much do the actors cost? Are they professional actors, or do they do acting as a hobby? Investing time here to get clarity will pay off.

What are your distribution rights?

There are different aspects in a video to consider that

influence the distribution rights. Music licenses, for example, are defined specifically for either internal use or online use, on your website, via pushed media, or on TV. Depending on the license agreement with the music distributor, your rights to the music in your video—and so your rights to repurpose the video or use it on another channel—may be limited. Make sure the license fits your needs. Agreements with actors are also very specifically defined. You may have the right to use your video internally only, or you could be allowed to show it on TV in a specific region for a specific time. Make sure these topics are thoroughly addressed. Get help from legal advisors if you have any concerns.

Can you keep the raw footage?

Once you have made the final payment, you should expect to hold full ownership of the video content—the footage that was used in your video. But make sure this is addressed. There may be additional footage that wasn't used, and you can negotiate for the rights to all the footage that doesn't appear in your video.

What is the pay schedule?

This should be addressed before you sign anything and definitely before you start production. Video production companies typically ask for at least a partial payment upfront.

PRINCIPLES

1. Work with a full-service video company that understands the creative process up to the distribution process.
2. Don't focus solely on quality; also consider the results.

TIPS

1. Carefully check the references of possible agencies.
2. Read or view testimonials from the company's current customers.
3. Look at their website's overall quality, not just the quality of their videos.

CHAPTER 6

THE PREPRODUCTION PROCESS

Putting your company's video on television or the internet for the world to see is thrilling, and you'll want to jump right in with the production! But first, you'll need to make sure you're fully prepared for production day.

Of the three steps in video production, *preproduction* is the most critical. While the *production* and *post-production* processes are fun and exciting, the success of your video depends on what you do *before* shooting starts. This is where you lock the idea, finalize the shooting script, align your budget, go location scouting, and complete all the planning. Think about *every* decision you have to make, and if you can do it now, do it! Eventually you have to make those decisions anyway, and if you're forced to make them under pressure—like during the shoot—you'll be more likely to make a bad choice. If you put off your decisions too long, it could be too late to make them at all. Take the time to talk through all your ideas and options with the production company and make every decision you can to leverage the power of your video to its fullest.

Meet with the video producers to talk with them about your business and discuss the story you want to tell. They need to understand your company and your message: who you are, what you do, and how you do it. They need to know about your value proposition, what makes you unique, and what you expect to achieve with your video. They also need to know your budget for production and distribution.

This will help you—with guidance from your producers—figure out how many videos you should make and can afford to make, the quality standard, where your target audience is on the customer journey, and where to place the videos. Be prepared to share openly and honestly so the producers can create a video that meets your expectations.

The preproduction process takes patience and should not be rushed. This is time well spent that will save you a lot of hassles down the road. Get your preproduction right, and you won't be scrambling to make costly and time-consuming adjustments later.

Before you start preproduction, you should have the concept approved by your leadership, if necessary, and a goal, a budget, a target group, and a general message, which you will fine-tune during the scripting process. Think about the production standard you wish to satisfy—the quality you need to achieve—and the potential channels where you might distribute your video.

If you don't have a firm budget, at least have a target amount to shoot for. As you go through preproduction, you can adjust it for costs that you didn't anticipate, such as a remote shoot or paid talent. Other factors marketers often don't anticipate that affect the budget include paid narration and adding animation, music, or a jingle.

Preproduction involves writing a script and may include location scouting and casting. Depending on the video, your producers might create a storyboard, shot list, shooting schedule, and call sheet. Some of these activities are internal to the production team and you won't see them, while others require your input. When you meet with the producers, ask them to explain their preproduction process so you know what to expect and can work closely with them to make your video a success.

THE BASICS

Have a clear outline of the project, beginning with (1) a

goal, (2) a target group, (3) key messages, (4) channels you're going to use, and (5) creative guidelines. Get these five things nailed down and keep them in front of you while you develop the story. Otherwise, they could get lost during the creative process. It's easy to get distracted and even forget what your initial goal was. You might end up with an awesome story that misses the target group or isn't right for your channels. So figure these out, write them down, and keep them front and center during preproduction.

WHAT IS THE GOAL?

Why are you making this video? What exactly is your goal with it? Be as specific as possible. Do you want to build trust? Do you want to explain how your product works? Do you want people to follow the call to action at the end? Communicating the goal to everyone involved in the process helps to make the video better. It can affect the story, the wording, the actors, and just everything else. Having a clear goal is the first and most important step in preproduction.

WHO IS THE TARGET GROUP?

Most likely your product or service is not for everybody. In order to capture your audience, you need to understand them and create a video just for them. Many clients struggle with describing their target group. Some are even afraid to identify one, because they think their product should speak to as many people as possible. That's not a good strategy. In today's world, there is a lot of noise with everyone trying to communicate with everyone else, so being specific is key to getting through to your audience. Speaking to a specific audience is how you get people to listen. It's like calling out someone's name in a crowd—that person knows immediately that your message is meant for them, and they turn to you to receive it.

Within your target, break down the group into individual personas if you can. Describe their character, their demographics, and their geographic locations as precisely as possible. Describe what their problems are and how your product solves those problems. This is very powerful and is key to connecting with your message.

WHAT ARE THE KEY MESSAGES?

The majority of advertisements lack clarity. If you don't believe me, do some web surfing and watch some video ads. Then try to decipher the key message. You can avoid this common mistake by defining your message upfront, in preproduction. If you have more than one message, decide which one is most important and make sure it's clearly communicated. If you have more than one message, fine. Prioritize them in a hierarchy and focus on the most important one when you create the story.

WHICH CHANNELS ARE WE PRODUCING THE VIDEO FOR?

Does it matter whether your video is going to be shown on social media or on your website? Yes, it does. People visit websites for a reason. They are warm traffic, actively looking for something. They will spend time on the site and are more likely to spend time watching your video than people on social media, who could scroll down or click away. Social media clips have to grab the person's attention right away, so they should be shorter and have an even more engaging opening. Before you decide on a channel or channels, understand the differences. Each social media channel has a different target group, so make sure you get the specifications for each beforehand. As a general rule of thumb, the further along a person is in the customer journey, the longer your video for that group can be.

WHAT ARE THE CREATIVE GUIDELINES?

In many cases, the only real creative guideline is the budget. Everything else is flexible. But you may have other requirements, like your video has to be shot at night or at a specific location. It might require certain actors.

Maybe you've already decided on a basic idea for the story. Whatever your creative guidelines are, get them out in the open right away. Write it down, discuss it with everyone involved in the decision-making, and share it with your production team.

TOP 5 QUESTIONS TO ANSWER IN PREPRODUCTION

1. What is the goal?

2. What is the target group?

3. What are the key messages?

4. What channels are we producing the video for?

5. What are the creative guidelines?

SHOOTING SCRIPT: THE STORY

The shooting script describes everything that happens in the video—the characters, images, dialogue, narration, and action. A good shooting script allows the director or the cameraman to direct and build each scene on the set. It requires powerful *visual* writing that's engaging, describes actions, and has words that are carefully chosen, with more verbs than nouns. It allows actors to prepare for the shoot and helps everybody involved. A full-service video production company will help you write a script that tells an engaging story that sticks—a memorable one that captures the audience to the end. In post-production, the editor will always have the script handy.

THE ENGAGEMENT MODEL

Following the engagement model to build your script ensures that the most important aspects are included. Think about it: everything shown in this model—authenticity, attention, target group, emotion and story, added value, and video length—influences the engagement with your audience and ultimately, the success of your video. Other factors affect its success, such as bad acting, bad lighting, poor video or sound quality, or the issues we talked about earlier such as cognitive overload, but using this model as a guide will help you avoid making major mistakes with your script.

The story you tell and how you tell it are the most important factors in creating a video that's believable and resonates with people. It should have structure, with a beginning, a middle, and an end. It should be authentic, take the customer's point of view into consideration, and give them what they need on their customer journey. A good story sparks emotion and is memorable. It's short and makes a point—like a sentence—and is never meandering or confusing.

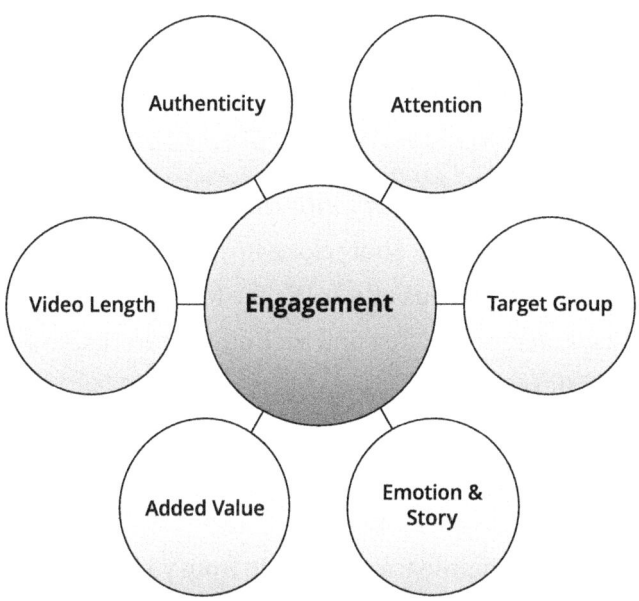

Refer to the Engagement Model When You Build Your Shooting Script

Attention

Grab the viewer's attention from the first second! The days of opening with a title are definitely over, and adding one won't help. Leave the title and description for the thumbnail. Instead, engage people quickly with sound, fast cuts that bring the story forward, by posing a question, or anything that arouses curiosity.

Target Group

Talk the way the target group talks, and the engagement will be higher. Use words they use and address problems they have.

Emotion and Story

Bring emotion and story into the video by building a story around people. Show close-ups whenever emotion is displayed. Famous editor Walter Murch's Rule of Six focuses on emotion first and then story. It works, so why do it differently?

Added Value

Will the audience learn something from your video, or is it just noise? Engagement will be higher if you educate your audience. Give them some insight and help them become smarter. Teach them something.

Video Length

Don't make a two-minute video when you can transmit your message in thirty seconds. The engagement will be significantly higher, and people won't miss the call to action at the end. Save your audience time and let them capture the *whole* story! The shorter, the better.

Authenticity

Go deep, be authentic. The world is full of artificial and superficial advertisement. If you transmit authentic content, you will immediately separate yourself from the rest. People love authenticity and will stick to your video—instead of clicking away.

USE CHARACTERS

The best stories are about characters. Human characters can make a story better in several ways:

1. A person in your video gives the audience someone to connect with and relate to and gives your story depth. The story might illustrate the person's challenges and motivations. This will arouse the audience's curiosity—they'll want to know more.
2. Characters in video marketing are powerful for their social proof effect. Have your protagonist show how your product works, and how well it works. A simple demonstration of the product leaves a lasting impression on your audience.
3. People are drawn to faces. Humans have neural circuits in an area of the brain called the fusiform gyrus that respond only to faces, so use them in your video marketing to draw and keep the attention of your viewer. Faces and facial expressions also convey a lot

of information and can evoke emotion in your viewer. They give your video an authentic look and feel.[20]

For your video to provoke action, it should connect with people on an emotional level. When you write your script, think about the emotions that you are appealing to in your story. The following blog from planner and strategist organization APG describes the six fundamental human emotions.

Cognitive neuroscience has identified six fundamental human motivations. These are the real emotional truths that get people to actually do something. If your brand can powerfully play to one of these motivations, you're in a good place. But first, you must know your target audience very well. When you sell children's safety seats, guess which motivation you *must* address? Security, of course. Your video can play to more than one motivation, depending on the persona. When you develop and review your script, be aware of your audience's motivations and address them properly.

1. **Security**: care, trust, closeness, security, warmth
2. **Enjoyment**: relaxation, fun, openness, pleasure
3. **Excitement**: vitality, fun, curiosity, creativity, change

---

20 Phil Nottingham, "Your Business's Videos Should Include Faces. Here's Why," *Wistia*, March 15, 2017, https://wistia.com/learn/marketing/power-of-faces-in-video.

4. **Adventure**: freedom, courage, rebellion, discovery, risk
5. **Autonomy**: pride, success, power, superiority, recognition
6. **Discipline**: precision, order, logic, reason[21]

STORY STRUCTURE

As you can imagine, not every story has the same structure. In video marketing, I recommend sticking to a linear structure. The following applies to every genre:

1. Get their attention at the start and build on that. Don't lose your audience.
2. Keep the flow going. Connect each step in the video.
3. Be clear! And remember that what's clear for you might not be clear for your audience.

The structure varies depending on the type of video you make—its genre. Following are the general formats to follow when structuring your video. Use these steps to build a story that makes sense to the target group and achieves your goal.

---

[21] Matt Willifer, "Practical tools and models," *APG: The Home for Planners & Strategists*, September 1, 2015, https://www.apg.org.uk/single-post/2015/09/01/Practical-tools-and-models.

Social Media Video or Explainer Video

Social media and explainer videos are ideally very short, and they make a point quickly. Grabbing the audience's attention right away is critical, especially with social media videos where the viewer finds your video by accident. They're not looking for it, and their attention span is limited. Follow these six steps for a strong social media or explainer video story:

1. **Introduction.** Make it brief. Get and hold the attention of your target group long enough to introduce the next step, the problem.
2. **Problem.** Describe the problem your product solves to connect with the audience.
3. **Meaning/Importance.** Make the problem important—like it's the biggest problem in the world. Continue to hold people's attention with this step.
4. **Solution.** Explain how your product solves the problem. Talk about your unique value proposition. This step is usually the longest in your video.
5. **Result.** Describe the benefits of using your product and how it improves the target group's lives.
6. **Call to Action (CTA).** Direct people to take the next step by clicking on a link to your website, calling you, or contacting you in some other way to order your product or service.

Testimonial, Customer Success Story, or Case Study

Testimonials, customer success stories, and case studies establish your credibility and build trust. Follow these six steps to create a structured, powerful, and authentic story that viewers can engage with.

1. **Introduction and Context about Your Customer.** Answer the questions "What do you do?" and "Who do you do it for?" Position yourself immediately so people understand how what you do relates to them in the story.
2. **Problem and Its Importance.** Answer the questions "Before you used the product, what was the problem?" and "What else did this problem affect in a deeper sense?" Connect with the audience by describing the problem and building up the value and importance of your product. Give specific examples, such as "Before we used this product, we didn't have time to do what was important in life, like spend time with our families (or visit our customers)."
3. **Trigger, or How the Customer Came to Use Your Product.** Answer the question "How did this customer hear about the product?" This is a short bridge between the problem and the next step, the solution.
4. **Solution.** The question here is "How does the solution work?" and the answer is your video showing the solution in action and visual proof that it works.
5. **Result.** "What are the benefits?" Describe the ben-

efits of the product and how it improves the target group members' lives.
6. **Call to Action (CTA).** Direct people to take the next step by clicking on a link to your website, calling you, or contacting you in some other way to order your product or service. Be sure to show your company logo and website URL.

Brand Video, Product Video, or Event Video

These genres work best with a simple EFC structure: E for Emotion, F for Facts, and C for Call to Action. Build up the story with emotion, addressing one of the fundamental human motivations. Then continue with an important and surprising fact about the topic or your product that grabs your audience's attention. At the end, finish up with a clear call to action.

1. **Connect with Your Audience.** Do this in an emotional way to engage them quickly.
2. **Explain.** Give people the facts about the brand, product, or event.
3. **Call to Action (CTA).** Tell people what to do next.

MODELING TECHNIQUES

Sometimes it's difficult to put into words what you want your video to look like. A script communicates only part of your message. The rest is transmitted by the colors, light, sounds, and even the motion principles you use.

Modeling techniques, where you find other videos, images, sounds, music, or anything that's similar to what you want your video to look, sound, or "feel" like, can be an effective communication tool to share with your team. Use other videos to quickly show the direction you want the video to go. Watching a video together that exhibits some of the aspects you're looking for takes the guesswork out of it. I may show a marketer several different videos that I think are similar to what they want so they can help me get closer to understanding their vision.

SOCIAL PROOF

People copy the actions of others. You might think you're behaving independently of those around you, but you're influenced by other people more than you realize. We display this behavior as children and repeat it throughout our lives. Psychology professor and author Robert Cialdini, in his book *Influence*, describes this psychological and social phenomenon as "social proof."[22]

Social proof is a powerful component of video marketing that you can incorporate into your script. Alex Kouts (@

---

[22] Robert B. Cialdini, *Influence: The Psychology of Persuasion* (Revised edition), New York: Harper Business, 2006.

akouts) is a teacher, adventure technologist, and chief product officer of political media company Countable. He's also—as you'll discover in his podcast "The Secrets You Don't Know About Negotiation Part Two"—quite savvy in negotiation, where he identifies five forms of social proof:[23]

1. Social Proof with Users, Consumers
2. Social Proof with Experts
3. Social Proof with Celebrities
4. Social Proof with Wisdom of Crowds
5. Social Proof with Friends

If you see a typical consumer use a product in a video, that's simple social proof. If the person using the product is an expert, the effect is stronger, and if the person is a celebrity, the effect is even more powerful. If a crowd is shown using the product, the social proof is stronger and its influence greater, and if the person is someone who you identify with as a "friend," the influence is more effective than ever. This friend doesn't have to be someone you actually know—it can be someone who just looks like the kind of person you'd hang out with or want to hang out with. This is why identifying your target audience is so important before you cast your video.

---

[23] Alex Kouts, "The Secrets You Don't Know About Negotiation Part Two," https://www.jordanharbinger.com/alex-kouts-the-secrets-you-dont-know-about-negotiation-part-two/.

Social proof also refers to actually showing your product in action—showing that it works and how it works. You can demonstrate a product or service, have a spokesperson show it working, or have a customer provide a testimonial about how it worked for them.

OTHER SCRIPT CONSIDERATIONS

Ten years ago videos were three or four minutes long. Today, people have many more videos to choose from and limited time to commit to each of them. Videos are much shorter now, so you have to connect and engage people fast.

Making a shorter video isn't easier than making a long one. Every decision you make counts: every word, every image, every note. So you have to have the courage to stand up for what's most important in your message and cut everything else. Position your business right away and tell your audience who you are and what you do immediately, so they know right away whether they should watch or click away. If you don't tell them, they will click away anyway.

Consider alternate approaches to creating video that speaks to your audience. One of our clients, for example, delivers financial insights from India. The fund manager frequently travels to that country to meet with companies and thought leaders, and she comes back with exciting stories to share with the target audience. We decided to teach her how to produce great content using only her mobile phone. This nontraditional approach allows her to produce engaging content while providing immediate firsthand insight to her audience. If you choose an approach like this, be sure that you know how to tell a story and communicate the story through video.

Don't sacrifice emotion to squeeze in a bunch of facts. Another business I worked with wanted to include a lot of facts in its video—so many it left no room for emotion. At most, people will only remember seven facts from your video, so put in the most important ones and cut the rest. That doesn't mean you have to throw all those facts away—they will probably work well on your website, where people can take some time to review them. In this instance, I recommended using only five facts in the video and then including a call to action to visit the company's website, where viewers could learn more, get all the facts, and order the product. When you try to cram too much in, people won't pay attention, and they won't remember what you said.

Finally, don't neglect the technical details. Tell your producer which channels you plan to use because that will affect how they shoot your video. For example, each social media channel has different target groups but might also have different technical requirements and different formats. Therefore, it is important to define the channels that are most critical to your distribution plan.

If people are going to watch your TV spot on a fifty-five-inch UHD television, you can show more details, including text. If they're watching on a desktop, those details will be lost, and on a mobile phone, all that text may be unreadable. The channels you use—along with your budget and the expectations of your company—affect the quality standard, and these all must be taken into account.

Also think about whether your video is targeting business to business (B2B) or business to customer (B2C) clients. Videos for B2C purposes are usually produced for mobile-first usage. That means the video, including the text, is optimized for smartphones. The text is easy to read, and there may be more close-up shots with fewer details than wide shots. These are cognitively easier to digest. Close-ups also tend to have a greater depth of field, making it easier for you to guide the viewer through your story. Mobile users will typically spend less time on your video than desktop users—another consideration when writing your script.

LOCATION SCOUTING

The script defines where the shoot takes place: in the studio, at the customer site, or somewhere else. Generally speaking, you'll have an easier time controlling the environment on an indoor shoot than one you do outside. If the shoot will be in your offices, find a clean, quiet location if possible. For legal reasons, you may have to cover the non-company logos on employee's clothing or cover artwork on the company's walls. Shooting video near a coffee machine or cafeteria invites interruptions and unwanted noises that may be impossible to remove in post-production and could delay the shoot. I speak from firsthand experience!

While you're writing the script, ask yourself if an outdoor shoot is necessary or if you could shoot the video indoors. If an outdoor shoot is required, you have more to think about, like a Plan B in case it rains. If you have a large cast and crew involved and you need to change plans, this could affect your budget and your schedule. Also think about the lighting. Is it better in the morning or the afternoon? You don't want to be shooting into the sun. The best light conditions usually occur when the sun is low on the horizon, in the morning or the evening. Discuss lighting with your production team before setting the schedule.

If you're shooting "on location," that is, outside of a production studio, visit the site ahead of time. Be aware of any background noise, and make sure you have permission to film there.

My team once did an onsite shoot inside one of the tallest buildings in Zurich. The shoot would take place in a huge, airy, light-filled room surrounded by high windows. We got to the site early to get all the lights, sound, and camera angles set up perfectly. It was a big production and we had planned everything ahead of time—or so we thought. Just as the shoot began, every window shade in the room closed. They were set up on an automatic sensor triggered by sunlight! It took time to find the only person in the building who knew how to override the electric shades and get them back open.

This was an important lesson for me in scouting a location. Whatever you don't expect to happen can and often will happen!

STORYBOARD

If the visual content is particularly strong or important, you might want to have a storyboard that shows the main visual images that will appear in order. Adding a storyboard affects your budget, because you'll need someone to draw each scene, but it can be especially useful if there is a lot going on visually and the timing is important.

Storyboards are more common in television commercial productions and big budget productions and less so in small- to mid-size company videos. If you think you need to see everything ahead of time, though, ask your producer for an estimate and get their opinion on whether they believe a storyboard is necessary.

YOUR CAST OF CHARACTERS

The people who appear in your videos can come from within your company, they can be your customers, or you can hire professional talent. For introduction and brand videos, it makes sense to cast company leadership and employees, and for testimonials, you will want to engage your actual customers. Using your own talent versus paid talent saves you money and transmits your message more authentically, but you'll want to give people time to practice and get comfortable speaking in front of an audience.

ACTORS

Another option is hiring an actor or actress. Acting comprises a wide range of skills, and I have a lot of respect for good actors. They know how to adopt a character and really dive deep into the role. Nuances in acting are small but can have a dramatic effect on the performance and how it's perceived by the viewer. Emotions are transmitted from actor to audience through facial expressions, body language, and voice inflections, among other things, and if the actor cannot get into the role, or if they sound like they're reading from a script instead of speaking from the heart, it's apparent. Test your talent and see how they look and sound on camera. Are they believable? If you don't want to use people from your business or actual customers, you can always hire actors.

Your video production company can either arrange the casting for you or work with a casting company where video castings are its daily business. These companies have an entire database of names, photos, and details of actors. Working together with a casting company and acting talents is expensive and, if you choose to go that route, will take up a big portion of your budget. However, depending on your story and your goal, I highly recommend using a casting company if you can afford it. Bad acting or unauthentic characters are the worst thing that can happen to your video marketing project. If you work with a casting company, be sure to specify *live* video casting. Don't settle for just an online selection of some portrait pictures. This way, you will get a good fit for your project.

VOICE-OVER ARTISTS

Get the right person to narrate your script. In very rare cases, this could be someone from the company, but I highly recommend hiring a professional voice-over artist.

A couple of years ago I used to invite voice-over talent into our studios to record their voices. We had to have a studio prepared and a sound engineer ready to manage the recording. The voice-over artist sometimes came from a distance away, such as Germany, and they traveled by train. Many hours were spent in the voice-over recording process.

Times have changed, and today getting a narration is much faster and easier. Today's professional narrator often has their own recording studio and can quickly deliver high-quality voice-overs, sometimes in just a few hours. The sound quality is amazing, and they even enhance their voice with personal optimized audio filters to deliver the perfect result. I love this! Sites like bodalgo.com even let you cast your narrator online from a list of talents and variety of languages.

Finally, speak with your producers about legal matters such as model releases and other rights and permissions that affect you and the people—such as your cast of characters and narrators—in your videos.

SHOT LIST, SHOOTING SCHEDULE, AND CALL SHEET

The shot list is typically an internal document for the production team and is simply a list of each shot the cameraperson or videographer is going to take. The list clarifies the shoot for the creative staff and helps avoid mistakes such as forgetting a certain shot. On the set, the creative staff is involved with so many aspects of shooting the film that it is very easy to forget something. The shot list usually contains scene number, shot number, location, shot description, shot size, and camera movement, such as pan, tilt, zoom, etc.

The shooting schedule gives the dates, times, and locations of each shoot. If you are shooting at a site that requires security checkpoints, like an airport, make sure you have worked all the access details out ahead of time and be sure to incorporate the extra time it will take into your schedule. If people from your company are going to appear in the video, they will need to know where to be and when to be there. Make sure the times do not interfere with their lunch or meeting times. If someone is in a meeting and you need them for the shoot, they could hold up the whole production team and throw off the schedule.

Whenever we have more than three crew members on a shoot, we use a call sheet. This is a one-page list of every important contact involved along with their phone number and the time, location, and address where they need to show up for the shoot. Weather forecasts and special set requirements may also be listed.

You may not be involved in creating the shot list, shooting schedule, or call sheet—or even see them—but knowing what they are makes you a more knowledgeable video marketer who can communicate more easily with your producers.

Approve each step of the preproduction process before moving on to the next step. This is critically important. If you are not thrilled with the script, don't allow a shoot to happen, thinking you can fix it later. *Communicate with your producer and tell them you need to approve each step.* They will be very happy to see you take this initiative, because it's always easier to get the video right the first time than it is to try and fix it later.

PRINCIPLES
1. Invest in preproduction to get the best results.
2. *Visualize* your video as much as possible. If you can't draw well, then describe it as visually as you can.

TIPS
1. Make your customer—not yourself—the hero of your story. Talk about them and their pains, problems, wants, and needs. That's what they care about and what will get them to listen to you.
2. If you are ever stumped about where to go with your

story, always go back to the customer journey. Who are the customers you want to reach right now, where are they in that journey, and what do they need from you?
3. If something is not clear, ask your production company for more details.

CHAPTER 7

THE PRODUCTION PROCESS

All that effort you put into preproduction pays off in the production process. Thanks to your dedicated involvement up to this point, you can hand the reins over to the people on your production team, confident that they understand what you want and are prepared to deliver to your expectations.

You might take days or weeks to plan your video during preproduction, but the actual shoot might take just a few hours or a couple of days. This is typically the easiest and fastest of the three stages of making a video. It's also the most physically demanding. Expect a big day. Rest up the night before and come to the production ready to work.

At this stage, you'll quickly discover how well prepared

you and the production team are for the shoot. If you did your preproduction homework, this step can be quite easy and even enjoyable. If not, you might end up at a shooting location that wasn't reserved, so you have nowhere to shoot. Maybe some crew members misunderstood the time and location, and they're back at the office wondering where everybody went. Soon it's lunchtime, and everybody wants to eat. Do you cancel the shoot, or order lunch and try to regroup? You can see how a lack of preparation could become a nightmare!

ONSITE AND LOCATION SHOOTING

In the days leading up to production day, communicate what's happening to the people at your company, especially if the video is going to be shot onsite. Let them know where and when you'll be shooting and whether they should avoid the area or if it's okay for them to walk through the shots. You may want to block off the area and put up signs to remind people that it's production day.

At least one person from your company, typically the director of marketing or other marketing specialist, should be the main point of contact for the visiting production team. That person will probably be you. Find out how much space the production people need for their vehicles and have a parking area reserved for them. If you have onsite security, let them know that you will have visitors, and if the production team needs temporary badges to get into your building, arrange for those.

For onsite shoots, meet them in the reception area of your business and give them a quick tour of your offices. Take them around the building and introduce them to anyone they may not have met yet who was involved in the pre-production. Your human resources representative may have done some behind-the-scenes work, and they will appreciate meeting the production crew and seeing how their efforts are contributing to the video. Introduce the team to all the stakeholders—the people who approved your budget and who have a vested interest in the success of the production—and to everyone who will be involved in the shoot that day.

A video shoot is exciting, and people will be nervous. The production team has a lot to manage: video cameras, lighting, sound—all the technical pieces of the shoot. The people who will be on camera are nervous, too, and you don't want people stressed out when they're being filmed, because that will come across in your video. Instead of jumping right into the shoot, give people time to calm their nerves and channel all that nervous energy into positive energy. Your production will go more smoothly if you allow everyone to shake hands, smile, get to know each other, understand each other's roles, and establish some trust.

After the introductions, show the production team the best entrance for bringing in their gear and where to set up. Show them where the restrooms and water fountains are, too. Let the producer talk through what will happen so everyone is prepared.

Expect to remain with the production team for the entire shoot. Some businesses require visitors to always be accompanied by a chaperone, but even if that isn't the case, stay with them to answer questions, support them with whatever they need, and help supervise the talent. If you have customers or people from your company speaking on camera, they may be tempted to improvise the script. This isn't a bad thing, and in fact unscripted testimonials often come across as more natural and authentic. In this instance, you would give the person a list of questions you're going to ask ahead of time and then just prompt them during the on-camera "interview." If you do this, make sure that whatever they're saying is acceptable. You or your communication representative will know this, but your producers may not. Then communicate with the producer, who will edit the video in post-production, keeping the best responses and cutting the rest.

If you have a company mission, vision, value statement, tagline, slogan, motto, or a value proposition that needs to be stated a certain way, make sure that whoever says it on camera knows it *exactly*. You might think everyone in your company knows the company's slogan by heart—trust me, they do not. I have video proof of this from some shoots!

People who aren't used to being filmed are insecure about how to behave in front of the camera. At the production site, we do everything we can to make them feel taken care of and comfortable. Plan time for a warm-up and to allow people to get to know each other. The talent, whether it's professional actors or your own employees, need time to get to know the crew. That time is valuable and can make a big difference in the overall performance of everyone involved.

It's common for people new to video to look straight into the camera. Unless this is in the script, they should avoid doing this, and you or the production team may have to remind them to look away. If you are shooting people working, give them a real task to do so they feel natural doing it. If you have people in the company who don't normally work together but are appearing on camera together, they should get introduced to one another before the shoot. If the camera captures them talking to each other without audio, have them explain what they are doing in their day-to-day work so the conversation looks natural and not staged.

Since you probably know the people on camera, help them

relax, but also feel free to talk to them about anything that doesn't show their best side. They will appreciate it. If their hair is sticking up, tell them—then give them time to fix it. If their shoulders are bunched up or they're sweating, kindly let them know. Production crews usually bring powder to subdue facial sweat and shine, so if you need help with the on-camera talent's appearance, ask for it. Don't be shy about giving your input! Any person who appears in your video will be very unhappy if you don't capture them at their best, so speak up *now* and save everyone any later grief.

Whoever is in front of the camera should want to be there. They should understand that this is about the customer and about showing their authentic self, as well as their products and services, to the people who are interested in what they have to offer.

You developed a strategy in preproduction, and when the videographer shoots your video, they should have a strategy, too. If you have questions about why they're doing things a certain way, just ask. Tell them to let you look in the camera viewfinder, too, so you can see what they're shooting. They will be happy to show you and explain everything to you. They want to get it right the first time—perhaps even more than you do—so if anything's off, it's up to you to let them know during production. Some things cannot be corrected in post-production.

Your producer may want to get what's known as a B reel, or B-roll footage. This is extra video that they can intersperse with the main shots. If you're shooting a testimonial, instead of showing the customer speaking into the camera the whole time, you can cut away to some B-roll video of them actually using the product or of people in the company designing and manufacturing it. If you're shooting a corporate video and the CEO is talking about the culture of the company, you might have some B-roll footage of people enjoying the company culture in the lunchroom, the company gym, or on a company picnic. Ask your production team to get whatever footage complements and visually enriches statements made within the narrative of your video.

A live shoot might take longer than expected, but you're better off taking the extra time to get people calm, comfortable, and confident on camera than rushing them and having a bad video of uptight people that you can't use. Video is fun. Make it fun.

STUDIO PRODUCTION

Not all of your production will be done onsite or at a location shoot. Sometimes you can shoot an entire video in the production company's studio. If you have a professional narrator or voice-over talent, the production company has a specially made sound booth and high-quality microphones and audio recording equipment.

If you are having a jingle or live music recorded, or having animation created, those extras will also be completed in the studio, or remotely, and your video production company can manage all the details for you. Be sure to talk through all this during preproduction so when production day comes, you'll get everything you envisioned for your video.

PRINCIPLES
1. Plan the day! Make sure you have a production schedule and enough time to complete it.
2. Show the protagonists and your site from the best perspective.

TIPS
1. Inform everybody in the company that you are making a video and reserve all the rooms and indoor and outdoor spaces you need in advance.
2. Make sure everybody feels comfortable. This is about your company, but it's about them, too!

CHAPTER 8

THE POST-PRODUCTION PROCESS

Now that you've shot your video, it's time to edit! This is where all your careful preproduction pays off. You've worked with your producers to create your story, and they've captured everything they need to make your vision come alive. The next step is putting all the pieces together to tell your story the way you want it told. Post-production is where the video magic happens.

A lot happens after the shoot, but most of it is on the production team. These people will have a short debriefing conversation with you and gather any outstanding graphics and guides and anything else they need to edit the video. They will work with the narrator or voice-over talent if you're using someone for that. They'll do the initial rough cuts for you to review and then do the fine cuts. They'll add all the graphics, audio, subtitles, and anything else you've defined in preproduction, too.

AFTER THE SHOOT

Right after the shoot, speak with the production team. Find out how they think everything went, good and bad. Some of the performers may have performed well while others did not. The lighting may have been less than ideal, or it may have been better than expected. The audio quality of the shoot may have been compromised—maybe there were unexpected interruptions from curious onlookers. This is a good time to get the producers' feedback and provide your own.

If you have any outstanding assets for the production, such as legal paperwork, your style guide, or marketing collateral, get it to the producers before they leave the site. If you're not onsite with them during the shoot, ask them to call you when they're done to let you know how everything went and to see if they need anything else to begin the editing process.

GRAPHICS, MOTION DESIGN, AND ANIMATION

This is a good time to revisit any graphics, motion design, or animation that will be incorporated into your video. Remember that all of these features should be defined in your company's style guide. Companies that start with video often forget this step. Don't make this mistake. If you're planning a production, reread chapter 2, "Take Inventory," and make sure you have done your homework. Invest a bit more time in your first video and get your video graphics right. Stick to your style guide. The colors and fonts used in post-production must match your guidelines. If you create lower thirds, intros, and outros, make them high quality and consistent with your style guide—you could be using and reusing them for many video projects over the years. If you produce videos on a regular basis, invest in some motion principles. This investment upfront will boost the overall perception of your videos.

That consistency in all your video marketing is extremely valuable. It helps your brand and saves you work, because you'll be able to repeat and reuse everything you define right now. Once it is set, everybody involved in the process knows what is expected.

RAW FOOTAGE

After a video shoot, your producers will have a lot of "raw footage." This is *all* the video they shot that will be used to create your finished video. If you get a first look at the raw footage, you may be surprised at how unfinished it appears. Don't worry—your producers shoot much more video than they need so they'll have several "cuts" of each shot to choose from.

After your producers review all the footage and select the best cuts, they'll process the video to improve its appearance. Producers can stabilize the video, optimize the saturation, and increase the contrast. For a high-quality production such as 4K, high definition (HD), or ultra-high definition (UHD), they may zoom in for some shots. After they process the video and add the music, graphics, and narration, you'll see how the different layers all come together to form the finished work.

VIDEO STORAGE

I often hear from my customers months and even years after I've produced their videos. They want to know if I still have all their videos and the raw footage. I typically hold onto clients' videos and footage for a while, but no production company will store your materials forever.

If you think you might want to use the raw footage for a future video project, ask your producers how long they save it. Don't assume they will maintain it after post-production. For a fee, they may provide you with a copy of the raw footage, or they may be willing to store it for you beyond their standard time limit. It's vitally important to consider this step, especially if you've had an elaborate or expensive production. You may have obtained model releases and legal forms and gotten permission to shoot at a particular site. You put a lot of time and effort into the production—you could use the raw footage for another video someday.

POST-PRODUCTION TIME: WHERE THE PUZZLE PIECES COME TOGETHER

The post-production process is done in the production studio, so you typically won't see all the work that goes into creating the finished video. If you'd like to see what happens during this process, ask your producers to invite you in for a quick tour. Even though you've already discussed all the details of your production, they may have more questions for you, too.

Of all the video and audio data gathered, only a fraction of it will be used. Sometimes we capture one and a half hours of video and audio footage for a ninety-second trailer. Then, it's like putting together a big puzzle. Every piece of it has to first be labeled, reviewed, judged, and put in its perfect place. Lots of content goes in the bin, of course. What appears at the end of the edit is true artwork built from carefully selected footage, together with a well-researched music title, a narration by a talented voice-over artist, graphics, and sound effects. Depending on the production outline, the final composition varies.

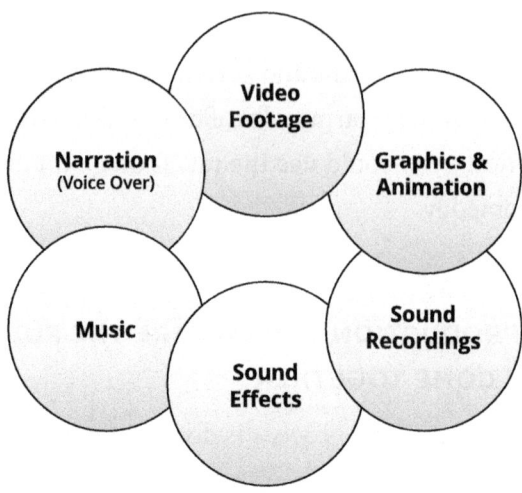

Post-Production Comprises Identifying the Right Elements and Fitting Them Together to Create a Perfect Puzzle

Post-production time varies depending on the length, complexity, and quality of your video, and your deadline. If you need a video in a very short time, your producers will typically meet your deadline, but they can probably create a better video for you with more time. You should discuss time estimates and deadlines with them during preproduction. At post-production, find out if they will still feel comfortable with the timeline.

Your producer will send you rough cuts at the beginning. These are unfinished video segments for you to view and provide feedback. They might ask you to come to the studio to see them, but more likely they'll send them to you digitally by a link to the video on a channel like

Vimeo. We use Vimeo review tools that allow our clients to provide feedback right in the video. The link is known only to you and them, so no one else can view it, and you can password protect it if you like. Your producer might also send you some audio samples for background music and narrator samples.

If you want your producers to finish in time, respond to them in a timely manner. You both have a schedule to meet, so if they send you something to approve, get to it as soon as you can. Delaying your response by days or even weeks holds up the process and interrupts the producer's editing process. With any creative endeavor, it's much easier to get back into the flow of the project within a short amount of time. If the post-production team has to step away from your project for weeks while they await a response from you, it will take them longer to re-engage with the work, and it may not flow as well. Keep the momentum going by having a schedule and sticking to it.

The best post-production happens because of a well-planned and executed preproduction. Despite all the wonders that can be done in editing, there is a lot that either you can't fix or you can but only with a lot of extra effort, time, and money. For your video to turn out great, nail the concept, the goal, the target audience, the positioning, and everything else that goes into preproduction first. Your producer takes everything you discussed and documented into the editing studio and takes it all into account during post-production, but if there are any questions left unanswered, the process will take longer and the results may not be what you expect.

While you're reviewing the video during post-production, return to everything you discussed in preproduction. Is your video going to attract your target audience? Is the right message coming through for wherever they are in their customer journey? How does the video feel? Does it build trust?

Think about it cognitively, too. Pretend you're an outsider who knows nothing at all about your company. Watch the video and see if it's clear. Do you understand the point it's making? How does it make you feel? Be honest in your appraisal. Now is the best time to get it right, not two weeks after you've spent a bunch of money promoting it.

TRUST YOUR POST-PRODUCTION TEAM

If you've vetted your production team and hired wisely, you should have nothing to worry about during this phase. Your video is in good hands with the professionals. If you'd like to learn about some of the thought processes and techniques that go on during post-production, I recommend the book *In the Blink of an Eye* by editor and director Walter Murch. His "Rules of Six" describe the critical points that drive his decisions in the video editing process. These are, in order of importance, the following:

1. Emotion
2. Story
3. Rhythm
4. Eye Trace
5. Two-Dimensional Place of Screen
6. Three-Dimensional Space

A discussion of these points is beyond the scope of this book, but you can read about them in Murch's book and then have an informed discussion about these techniques with your producer, especially if you feel any of these are lacking in the video.

> "If you have to give up something, don't ever give up emotion before story. Don't give up story before rhythm, don't give up rhythm before eye-trace, don't give up eye-trace before planarity, and don't give up planarity before spatial continuity...The ideal cut is one that satisfies all the...six criteria at once."[24]

Even though your production team watches your video over and over again, and you watch it over and over again,

---

24 Walter Murch, *In the Blink of an Eye: A Perspective on Film Editing*, 2nd edition (West Hollywood: Silman-James), 2001.

don't be in a hurry to promote it. Have several people at your company view it, set it aside for a day, and look at it again. Editing is tricky work, and it's very easy to miss errors in the work.

Invite people from your target audience to watch it. They might not be familiar with your product or services and can give you important feedback. They can tell you if they got the message and whether something is unclear. I take every viewer's comment seriously. Listen to the feedback—dive in and try to understand it from their perspective.

PRINCIPLES

1. Emotion and story come first.
2. Be ready to cut out a lot. Focus on the important.
3. Be clear about the messages!

TIPS

1. If you watch the video, put yourself in the perspective of the target audience. What do they know, and what don't they know?
2. Ask yourself: Can the audience absorb and understand everything?

ACT III

DISTRIBUTION AND WHAT COMES NEXT

CHAPTER 9

YOU HAVE A VIDEO: NOW WHAT?

Recently, I met with a CEO in the aesthetics industry who was struggling to get new customers, and he wanted to attract business with some new marketing. He decided to use Instagram as his main channel. This strategy didn't make sense to me with his proposed budget. Using social media—any social media—requires constantly feeding your audience new content. And the content, whether it's images, text, or video, is short-term. The audience isn't warm—you're reaching cold traffic at the beginning of their journey, where they are not even aware of you. They're far from being ready to buy. So you have to cultivate them over a very long period of time.

Every video you make requires your time and your budget. It takes energy. Think carefully about how you're going to expend all that energy. Do you want to use it up fast or make it last? I spoke to this man about his plan and offered him some other options. I looked at his website and realized he wasn't doing everything he could to attract prospects and customers throughout their customer journeys. His site had an attractive design, but he wasn't using SEO to get people to it—in fact, on a Google search of his specialty, his company didn't even appear on the first page of results, or the second, or the third. It was on the fourth page! Ninety-two percent of Google search traffic comes from page one—the first ten results of a search. So if you are on page two or later, the odds of being selected are very small—8 percent or less![25]

Marketers often think the solution to their marketing problems is social media, without understanding all the potential they already have or understanding how to leverage social media the right way—to drive traffic to their website—for long-lasting results. Which has the better payoff: a short-term campaign in social media that's out of sight and out of mind after a week, or a customer journey strategy that incrementally communicates with people every step on their way to becoming repeat customers?

---

25 Jessica Lee, "No. 1 Position in Google Gets 33% of Search Traffic [Study]," *Search Engine Watch*, June 20, 2013, https://searchenginewatch.com/sew/study/2276184/no-1-position-in-google-gets-33-of-search-traffic-study.

I advised this client to work on his website's SEO first, create videos for his site that met his audience where they were on their customer journey, and finally engage a multichannel strategy that included social media to drive traffic to his company site.

I never told him to stop thinking about social media or give up on it altogether, but if he wanted real results, he had to put it on the back burner and prioritize other channels first. My client understood, and a few tweaks to his website and better keyword optimization improved his SEO immediately. With considerably less effort than it would have taken to post to Instagram every day, we got instant results. Then we created a terrific brand video for his main page. Now he's busy creating more videos for each stage on the customer journey.

Producing a great video is the first part of your video marketing implementation. Getting it out there in a way that's sustainable for you and lasting for your audience is just as important. You should consider distribution in preproduction because where and how you get it to your audience affects your budget and the production. Distribution is part of the whole strategy for achieving your marketing goals.

A Hollywood movie might cost $200 million to produce, and the studio might spend more than $200 million more on marketing. Think about your video the same way. You don't have to spend as much as you did for the production, but if you want results, you can't ignore the distribution either.

> "Many marketers know they should be using video strategically, but often create video content to simply check off a box."[26]

Your video marketing strategy includes a distribution strategy, and it should match the implementation strategy you selected in chapter 4, "Strategies for Implementing Video." Before choosing a strategy, though, let's talk about three distinct *types* of video marketing channels: owned, paid, and earned.

You can use any or all of these types of channels in your strategy but ultimately, your decision will depend on your budget, your goals, and your target groups, and where they are in the customer journey.

OWNED, PAID, AND EARNED MEDIA

At the beginning of the customer journey, your target audience is not aware of you. You don't have anyone's attention and no matter how spectacular your first online

---

26 Jenny Mudarri, "The Wistia Guide to Video Marketing," *Wistia.com*, March 15, 2018, https://wistia.com/learn/marketing/video-marketing-guide.

videos are, you are competing with the entire internet. You need a way to get your videos in front of these people.

Content marketing distinguishes between three different online exposures for posting your content and videos. Often, your strongest strategy depends on a mix of two or all three types. Briefly explained, here are examples of each: Your video on your website is *owned* media, your video in a YouTube bumper ad is *paid* media, and an expert blog that publishes your video is *earned* media.

OWNED MEDIA

Owned media refers to channels that you control. These include your website, blog, and mobile site; dedicated YouTube channel; social media pages like Facebook, Twitter, and Instagram; and your newsletter. Content on your owned media builds long-term relationships with your prospects and customers and can be repurposed or shared by your audience via "earned media," which I will describe shortly.

Owned media is cost-effective, and you have complete control over it. Its longevity and versatility work to your advantage because you can change the content, including your videos, as frequently as you like and leave it in place as long as you like. Owned media is ideal for reaching niche markets that are researching a specific product or service that you deliver. The challenges with owned media are that there are no guarantees that anyone will see your content. They have to know about your site or be searching your company or products to find it. Also, company communication is not always trusted. It takes time to scale an audience by marketing only through owned media, but still it is a vital channel for all your content, including video.

You can deliver video content to your newsletter subscribers and specify which videos you send based on the customer's position on their journey. If they just bought a new product that requires setup or installation, send them an explainer-of-installation video. Show them how to use the product and examples of people using it in different ways that bring value. Include contact details so they can reach out to you for additional assistance. Make it easy for them to ask questions, order extra parts, hire someone to install the product, or order add-ons.

If you are having an event around your company's products and services, invite customers with videos on your social media and in your newsletter. Video record the event so you can show everyone who attended what a great time they had and remind everyone who missed it to be sure to attend the next event. The flexibility and low distribution cost of owned media allows you to experiment with video marketing without worrying about blowing your budget, and if something isn't working, you can simply take it down or replace it with another video.

PAID MEDIA

To get people to see your owned media, you can use paid media as a catalyst to drive people to your website and to other channels or landing pages that you control. Paid media takes advantage of an existing channel like YouTube or LinkedIn that already has the attention of your company's target audience. You have to pay to post your videos in these channels.

You can run your paid videos on video channels that cater to your audience as short video advertisements that preface the videos people intentionally click on. The viewer typically has to watch the paid media before the owned media content—the stuff they clicked on to see—appears.

A strategy of pushing content through paid media gets fast results because you don't have to spend a lot of time cultivating an audience. You can place paid videos on YouTube, news sites, social media sites like Facebook, professional networking sites liked LinkedIn, and any other site that accepts paid media. Your video can be as short as six seconds and as long as a minute. You can pay to have the viewer click through the video after a certain number of seconds or pay to have them view the entire video before the owned content appears.

Paid media also includes TV spots, or commercials. Online paid media can be placed to target a specific audience, whereas television spots tend to reach a much broader audience. The ability to reach a narrow, targeted audience is powerful—especially when you're a B2B company trying to reach other businesses with your products. Paid media allows you to get in front of your target audience and scale up that audience more quickly than relying simply on owned media. However, like owned media, people do not always trust paid media. You're also competing with a lot of other online media for the attention of your viewer. It's no surprise, then, that response rates for paid media have been declining.

EARNED MEDIA

When your customers become the channel, you are the benefactor of earned media. This happens when people share your content. Basically an example of word of mouth marketing, earned media creates a buzz, and your videos may even go viral, reaching hundreds of thousands or even millions of viewers.

You can't run earned media or pay for it. If you could, everyone would be doing it because it's very credible and plays a key role in sales. Earned media can have a very long shelf life, as it's shared and re-shared. However, earned media is often the result of a well-planned, well-executed, and well-coordinated video marketing campaign of both owned and paid media.

While earned media is powerful and generally positive, you have no control over how it is perceived by the public. You may have produced a video that misses the mark so badly it goes viral for all the wrong reasons. Think of a CEO or other leader who responded to a serious product issue, via social media, with a canned and cold response. That response may be shared or retweeted thousands of times, and because it's out there on the internet, damage control will be next to impossible. Those words could be out there for eternity. For this reason, using owned and paid media to generate a buzz requires a well-thought-out plan. Finally, since you have so little control over earned media, its results are difficult to measure.

DISTRIBUTION STRATEGIES

Again, the distribution strategies align with the four video implementation strategies described in chapter 4: Single Video Strategy, Customer Journey Strategy, Campaign Strategy, and Cultivation Strategy.

SINGLE VIDEO DISTRIBUTION STRATEGY

The single video distribution strategy is a good solution for tackling issues around branding, installation, service, or any other topic that you have identified as requiring quick communication with your audience.

In this strategy, your primary channel is your company's website. You can place your video on your company's dedicated video platform—YouTube, Vimeo, or Wistia—and then embed it on your landing page. Make sure your website is up to par as far as content, design, function, and SEO before you put the video on it.

This "quick fix" strategy is a low-cost way to fix a problem that needs immediate attention. But be aware, it is only a low-cost solution *as long as you have a minimum amount of traffic to your site*. Without enough visitors, this strategy won't help so make sure your website's SEO is up to date.

The single-video distribution strategy works well long-term. You can get even more mileage out of the videos with paid ads that drive traffic to your website, where your target audience can learn a lot about you by viewing your video. The only downside is that you only have one video, so you can only address one issue or talk about one product.

CUSTOMER JOURNEY DISTRIBUTION STRATEGY

This strategy also relies on your website for distribution. Like the single video strategy, place your videos on YouTube or another video platform and embed them into your website. The difference here is that you produce videos for each stage of the customer journey, so you could have videos on many different pages on your site. The production costs will be higher, but distribution costs will still be low.

Again, make sure your website's content, design, function, and SEO are in good order and that your servers can handle the traffic before you embed videos on it.

The customer journey distribution strategy is the perfect long-term strategy for communicating with your prospects, new customers, and existing customers. The one downside is that you are marketing through just one channel—your website—but you can boost the effectiveness of this strategy by constantly working on your SEO. One way to do this is by posting valuable, quality blogs that are relevant to your target audience. You can also combine this approach with paid ads that drive people to your website and videos.

CAMPAIGN DISTRIBUTION STRATEGY

The campaign strategy is typically short term and used to

generate interest in a new product or service or an event. It's also famously used for political campaigns. For the best results, implement a multichannel strategy with paid media on channels such as YouTube, any social media such as Facebook or Instagram, and television.

Constantly review the results such as click rate and conversion on all the channels. Make reliable adjustments and use A/B testing to increase effectiveness. You can measure the responses quickly and adjust the strategy on the fly for optimal results.

The production of a campaign distribution strategy usually includes several videos or different lengths, optimized for each channel. The production and distribution costs are much higher, but this is *the best method* for fast results.

CULTIVATION DISTRIBUTION STRATEGY: THE GROW YOUR AUDIENCE STRATEGY

YouTube is the primary channel for growing your audience. With this strategy, you post new videos regularly and often to your dedicated YouTube channel, targeting a very specific audience.

With the cultivation distribution strategy, your videos must bring value every time, and there is little room for error. Since you are building an audience of subscribers, people will have an expectation, and you have to deliver. This can be time-consuming, so you'll need at least one dedicated resource—a full-time person or a third party—to manage the production, distribution, measuring, and analysis of your videos.

CHOOSING THE RIGHT SOCIAL MEDIA CHANNEL

The "expiration date" of marketing channels varies from years to minutes, with social media posts at the short end of the spectrum. A Facebook post's shelf life averages five hours, while your Twitter post is good for just eighteen minutes![27] So your post from two weeks ago—or even two *hours* ago—may already be outdated. In order to be successful, you must constantly be posting, and the content must be valuable. This can be very time consuming.

Another way to reach your goals is with very targeted, paid, *measurable* ads on social media. Target different audiences with your videos, compare the results, and continuously improve your distribution groups. Always employ a multichannel strategy so you can continue comparing results and making improvements to your videos and how you target your audience.

---

27   Breanne Liebmann, "How Long Does Content Last and How Frequently Should You Post on Social Media?" *Sprocket Websites*, June 28, 2018, https://www.sprocketwebsites.com/Blog/how-long-does-content-last-and-how-frequently-should-you-post-on-social-media.

A chart published on Khoros recommends using specific networks, or online platforms, to reach audiences in retail, media, sports, consumer packaged goods (CPG), financial services, automotive, and health care industries.[28]

When selecting your channels, consider the demographics of your target groups on their customer journey. Look at which channels attract your market. Keep in mind that what you read about the demographics for channels isn't always correct, and it is always changing. No marketer or internet expert can predict with 100 percent certainty where your video marketing will perform best, but there are tendencies and trends among the different channels regarding age group, gender, and income. Choose a few channels that you believe best suit your audience and test them yourself. Serious distribution doesn't happen unless you are testing, measuring, and constantly improving!

A/B (SPLIT) TESTING

Comparing the results of different versions of a video, or of the same video on different channels, helps you make informed decisions about which videos to run and where to focus your budget. You can do this with A/B, or "split," testing.

---

[28] "2018 Social Audience Guide," *Khoros.com*, https://assets.khoros.com/content/tipsheets/2018-Social-Media-Demographics-Spredfast.pdf.

With A/B testing, you produce two or more versions of the same video, each with different variables, and test them on one channel. You might have a male talent on one and a female talent in the other, but everything else is the same. Or you could have the same female talent in both videos and change up the script. You can compare just about anything: different music, lighting, pacing, narrator, and more.

An alternative is placing a video on two or more different channels and measuring the results to see which channel gives you the most clicks, conversions, and so on. Since costs to use different channels vary, you can use this knowledge to determine your cost per conversion.

Facebook allows you to test many variables, including still images versus video. To learn more, check out its Split Testing & Test and Learn page at https://www.facebook.com/business/help/1962159924052051?helpref=faq_content.

The video platform Wistia also allows for A/B testing with video. YouTube does not have this functionality as of this writing, but a solution from Vidvision can be incorporated to do this type of testing with your YouTube videos.

Video distribution is a complex field, and you may be better off hiring a professional to do it for you while you're learning. Your full-service production company can get you started and may even offer distribution as a service.

VIDEO SEO BEST PRACTICES

While there are no guarantees that any one channel will perform to your expectations, you can make it easier for your prospects and customers to find you by enlisting a few simple best practices. For YouTube, we also use a browser plug-in called Videolytics from TubeBuddy that detects and suggests opportunities for better visibility, such as uploading a high-resolution thumbnail or adding info cards.

Once you've installed your YouTube channel and uploaded your video, follow these steps to make your video more visible. These work for YouTube—the second largest search engine—and any other video platform.

Improve the Effectiveness of Your YouTube Video Marketing with Best Practices

1. **Create a relevant title** that grabs the attention of your audience quickly. Even more importantly, make sure the title contains relevant keywords that your targets are looking for. Ideally, the title should be no more than 70 characters long. Get familiar with the free Google Ads tool Keyword Planner and figure out which words people are searching for.
2. **Add a description.** The description has a limit of 5,000 characters on YouTube but about 250 words or less will do the job. Most search engine results will cut the text at around 100 to 120 characters. Make sure the description also contains the keywords that are in the title at least once. On top of that, add links to your website and to all your social media accounts.
3. **Use subtitles or captions** on your videos. Subtitles or captions enhance the user experience, so YouTube and other video platforms will reward you with a better ranking. Your video production company can do this during post-production, or you can add them yourself with a tool on YouTube.
4. **Design a great thumbnail in high resolution.** Think of your thumbnail like the cover of a magazine—people decide whether to open it based on that single image. Having a picture of a face on your thumbnail can increase the click rate by as much as 25 percent.[29] Your thumbnail might have some text that attracts

---

29 Phil Nottingham, "Your Business's Videos Should Include Faces. Here's Why," *Wistia*, March 15, 2017, https://wistia.com/learn/marketing/power-of-faces-in-video.

your audience, or it might pose a question that makes them curious. Don't make the text too long, though—three to six words are plenty! Remember, many of your customers are looking at videos on their smartphones. The website canva.com offers a great way to create amazing high-quality thumbnails in a matter of minutes if not seconds. It will also convert your thumbnail into the right format.

5. **Research and implement tags.** YouTube tags are a great way to leverage your visibility. Also here, as in the title, use the Keyword Planner tool to evaluate the best tags. Be aware, they also have to be relevant to your video topic. Order them according to their importance.

6. **Implement info cards and end screens.** They are perfect for engaging with your audience and help to further improve the visibility of your video on YouTube.

7. **Share your video on social media.** Every Like, every Share, and every Comment on your video will prove to YouTube that your video matters. Share your video on as many channels as possible to get the greatest results.

8. Wherever you put your videos, make sure you also **embed your videos into your website.** This is where people will find them at each step of the customer journey. Put them on the right pages so no matter where people are on their journey, they will get the

right message. This will also help to enhance the YouTube engagement and view count.

9. **Keep an eye on the results.** After you have done your homework and implemented these best practices, don't get comfortable. Always keep an eye on the performance on YouTube such as the view count and the engagement. Find out which videos and topics perform best and constantly keep improving your video marketing.

PRINCIPLES

1. Even the best video is worthless without distribution.
2. Multichannel strategy is best for results.
3. Use video SEO best practices.

TIPS

1. Invest in distribution according to your strategy.
2. When in doubt about where to invest resources, invest in your website SEO first.

CHAPTER 10

SMART DISTRIBUTION: TRACK, MEASURE, ANALYZE, AND LEVERAGE RESULTS

Your website is the primary channel for reaching people at every stage of the customer journey. It goes without saying, then, that collecting and measuring website traffic data provides you with the most critical information to guide your video marketing efforts.

Analyze your website's video marketing data and pay special attention to its relationship with conversion. Which pages and videos are people viewing when they decide to buy from you, converting from prospect to customer? These correlations are invaluable for making informed decisions that drive conversions.

Likewise, measure and leverage the data from your pushed (paid) media on YouTube. To be honest, most of our clients start thinking about video analytics only after we address it. Yet it's a proven method for constantly improving your video actions. Analytics are especially useful when you have several videos in your pipeline and you can compare the strengths and weaknesses of each one. This is very powerful and can boost your video success fast.

ESTABLISH A BASELINE WITH ANALYTICS

Begin with discovering the status quo—what do your website's stats look like before you implement a video marketing effort? If you haven't already, talk to your web developer about collecting data by installing Google Analytics to analyze it.

Google Analytics allows you to track all website user data that is relevant to you. You gain an overview that allows you to understand any changes that you undertake on your website, such as putting up a new video on a certain page. To get started, you'll need an analytics account and a tracking ID. This has to be installed on your website. Ask your web admin to install it for you and deliver a monthly report.

Measure the number of visits and unique visitors to your site, which pages they visit, and how long they stay on each page. Measure the bounce rate, or percentage of visitors who leave your site after viewing just one page. Find out where your traffic comes from geographically and the percentages of people accessing your site via desktops, versus tablets, versus mobile devices like smartphones. Once you've established a baseline, you can implement your videos on your preferred video platform and begin to measure the impact on your website results. Your video platform—YouTube, Wistia, or Vimeo—can also give you heaps of different metrics.

SET GOALS

Set some goals that you'd like to reach with your video implementation. Look to your challenges or problem areas and look at what you want to achieve. Then think about the goals you'd have to reach to help you with those issues or achievements. You might want to increase the following numbers:

- Visits, unique visitors, or time spent on your site or on a particular page by a certain percentage.
- People who use your explainer videos instead of calling your tech support line.
- People who subscribe to your newsletter.
- People who provide you with their contact information to get something in return, such as a free sample or a PDF of valuable content.

- People who convert from prospects to customers by making a purchase.

Make your goals specific and set a time limit. For example, put a paid video ad on LinkedIn and set a goal to attract 1,000 new newsletter subscribers within three months.

MEASURE RESULTS

Whether you are a B2B (business to business) or B2C (business to customer) company affects your results in several ways. B2B traffic to your site typically originates from desktops because people visit from their offices. B2C traffic commonly comes from mobile devices because people surf the web and search for products on their phones while they're on the go or relaxing at home on the sofa.

Tracking the traffic will show you which pages get the most visitors and if your website is attracting your target groups. It will show you which pages people are most likely to navigate away from, which tells you that maybe you need to add an easy and enticing way for them to visit more pages. Short visits may indicate that your content isn't engaging people or delivering the value they're looking for.

Relevant, engaging videos can increase the number of

visits and time spent on your site, which in turn raises your rating on Google so your site is more apt to turn up, and appear higher on the results page, in an internet search. Videos boost your SEO, so you're more likely to be found.

MEASURE AND ANALYZE TRAFFIC TO YOUR VIDEOS

Google Analytics measures your website's user data, but it won't tell you anything specific about whether anyone watched your videos. However, the platform where you place your video, before you embed it into your website, can provide that data in its analytics section.

Our preferred platforms, such as YouTube, Vimeo, and Wistia, have different objectives, which you should evaluate against your goals. Wistia is the most powerful for marketers and, at the time of this writing, the only one that offers A/B testing. Unlike YouTube or Vimeo, it's not a platform for hosting videos that people can find with a search but rather a place to host your videos, embed them into your site, and have access to powerful measuring tools. Video platforms track who watches your videos and for how long, and more. For example, Wistia offers detailed views of the point in the video where people stopped watching and whether they watched a certain point in your video more than once.

Think about how useful this information is for, say, a tutorial video. If most of your viewers are pausing twenty seconds in and going back to something that happened at fifteen seconds, maybe the content in that portion of the video needs to be explained more clearly or presented more slowly.

If you post a three-minute video and 80 percent of your viewers stop watching at two minutes, either they lost interest at that point or your video is simply too long. You can look at the point at which people tune out and see what needs to be changed in your video to keep people engaged, or decide to shorten it.

Vimeo also has some of this functionality, although not to such a granular degree. YouTube may not have the customization abilities of these other platforms, but as the number two search engine in the world, it's the most popular and has its own advantages when it comes to reaching a big audience. YouTube is free, and you can access the Creator Academy to constantly improve your YouTube knowledge. Wistia loads faster than Vimeo or YouTube, so your page's loading time is shorter. This platform also allows you to implement countless lead generation tools from email collection to annotation links in order to grow your audience and reach your marketing goals faster.

Once you decide which platform to use, stick with it so

you can measure trends over time. It's very difficult to measure data across multiple platforms, so choose the one that's within your budget, does what you need, and that your web analyst or programmer can manage.

Video Platform	YouTube	Vimeo	Wistia
Advantages	• Second largest search engine • More than a billion users • Ideal for gaining many subscribers	• More design options • Match your content strategy	• Fast-loading player • Best analytics tools • Great customer support
Disadvantages	• Inferior video compression and quality • Limited engagement tools (you cannot request email addresses in the video) • Limited design	• Subscription is required for access to advanced tools	• More expensive, so geared for larger companies that run a lot of videos
Remarks	• Has its own video editor/editing tools • Accepts paid video ads on its platform	• Three video plans: pro, business, and premium	• Connects to marketing tools like HubSpot, Marketo

WHAT TO MEASURE

Video measurements come with a language that you've probably heard but may not understand. I'll list some of the most common data points that you should track and analyze. You will probably discover more as you start using all the tools available on various channels.

- **Impressions** are how many times your video appears in front of an audience.
- **Click rate** or **play rate** is the number of times someone actually clicks on it, represented as a percentage of impressions. If someone clicks on the video and it starts, it counts, even if they immediately click away from it.
- **Views** are how many times someone actually watches the video. Different platforms count views differently, so you can't combine the numbers and get an accurate result. Facebook and Instagram count a view after just a few seconds, while YouTube doesn't count it unless the video runs for at least thirty seconds. Views are an important measure, but they're not everything. To get a lot of views, you need a strong platform with a lot of visitors, so it helps to use paid ads to increase traffic to your videos if you want to increase your views.
- **Engagement** refers to how long someone stays on your video. If most visitors click away after a few seconds, you have an engagement problem. Maybe your video isn't interesting or exciting, or maybe it misses the mark when it comes to your audience. Engagement and play rate tell you a lot about the effectiveness of your video—whether you positioned yourself correctly with the right message to the right

people. Shorter videos can help with engagement—people may not want to watch a video that lasts two minutes, but they will watch a ten-second video. Consider this if you're thinking about producing a two-minute video—why not make two one-minute videos instead? An added advantage to a high engagement rate is that it will boost your Google rating.
- **Conversions** are the number of times someone takes an action. This is also represented as a percentage of either the clicks or impressions. Conversions can refer to people who respond to a video by going to your site, subscribing to your newsletter, or making a purchase. You define what conversions are for your business. Increase conversions with a call to action at the beginning, middle, and end of your video.
- **Shares, comments, and retweets** show you if you are reaching the right audience, and whether there is interest in your message.

Tracking these numbers gives you the data you need to make adjustments to your distribution strategy. Methods like A/B testing give you even more information, so if you have the budget, consider adding them to your strategy. You might be paying a lot for distribution on a channel that's giving you a high click rate but a low conversion rate, while at the same time you're paying much less on a channel where you're getting fewer clicks but a much higher conversion rate. Where do you think you should be putting your budget?

These are the kinds of things I look at when measuring and testing distribution strategies. A product video I produced recently got 30,000 views in just two days. Another video my company produced and ran in three languages ended up with three million views. With that many views, the businesses weren't as concerned about click rates and conversions, because even a small percentage would have yielded a great response. Still, we measured and analyzed it, and so should you.

Finally, you can look at how your results line up with your goals. If you ran a video with the intention of reaching people at a particular point on their customer journey, are those the people who converted? If you were trying to reach a certain demographic, is that who responded? You can see how complex measuring video can be. You can make it as simple or as complicated as you want, as long as you have the resources to support it. Once you have a solid website, have optimized it, and have populated it with videos, start pulling the data and analyzing it. Measure it and see what it tells you. Use what you learn to improve your video implementation and measure the results. Each time you change it up, learn a little more about testing and measuring, and when your results are powerful enough to warrant a dedicated resource to manage this, consider hiring a specialist or outsourcing it. Or just learn how to do it yourself and become the in-house expert!

PRINCIPLES

1. Conversion is the most important measure of results. Place a clear call to action within your video—what they need to do to become your customer. This can be a phone call, email, or going to your website. If the call to action drives people to your site, make sure you have a contact form that's easy for your audience to locate and complete, an easy way for them to subscribe to your emails, and a prominently placed phone number so they can call you.
2. Constantly improve your strategy and your videos by surveilling your video key metrics.

TIPS

1. Measure different videos against each other. The video platform Wistia offers A/B testing.
2. Most of your competitors don't measure or analyze their data properly. Do it right, and you will be ahead of the curve.
3. Put your videos high on your website so people don't have to scroll down to find them.
4. Always use best practices to improve your measurements and video performance.

CHAPTER 11

TOP 15 VIDEO MARKETING MISTAKES TO AVOID

When people come to me for video marketing, I take the responsibility as seriously as if I were producing a video for my own company. I want to present their businesses authentically and help them get the results they're looking for.

Sometimes this means slowing people down and getting them to take a little more time to think about what they want to accomplish. Then we can discuss the best way to make it happen. They may have certain expectations or assumptions due to inexperience, and it's up to me to educate them and guide them in the right direction. This means having honest discussions, listening to one another, and working together to avoid the pitfalls many new video marketers make.

I've put together a list of mistakes I see video marketers make most often. These aren't accidents—they're actions and decisions that are all within your control. As you venture into video marketing, check in with yourself and your producers along the way. Compare your progress with this list to ensure you're not making these common mistakes. With proper preparation, clear expectations, and diligence throughout the process, you'll get what you want and expect from video marketing.

MISTAKE #1: CHOOSING THE WRONG VIDEO PRODUCTION COMPANY

This happens when you're in a hurry to make a video and go with the first production company that seems to be able to do what you want. Don't settle when it comes to choosing your production team. Look at their website and their videos. Talk to their customers. Meet with the production team and find out if they understand important concepts such as customer journey, story, content strategy, and distribution strategy.

Make sure their mission and values align with yours. They should know something about marketing and not simply be in the video-making business.

MISTAKE #2: FAILING TO DEFINE A CLEAR GOAL

Know what you want to accomplish with your video. Maybe you want more people to get more value from your company's website. That's a broad goal, but it gives you the direction you need to create more specific goals to help you achieve it.

Make S.M.A.R.T. goals that feed into your overall goal. Think about what has to happen for more people to get more value from your website, and make each of those goals Specific, Measurable, Achievable, Relevant, and Time-based. Here are some examples:

- Increase visits to your website by 15 percent within one week of launching the video.
- Increase average visit times to your site by fifteen seconds within one month of launching video.
- Increase number of conversions on your site by x.
- Increase number of sales by x.
- Increase value of sales by x.

MISTAKE #3: NOT UNDERSTANDING AND DEFINING THE TARGET GROUP

A clear goal that's tied to the customer journey will determine who you need to reach, where to find them, and the story you need to tell them. Understand who your target group is. What moves them emotionally? What problems do they encounter at this stage in the customer journey? Do they need more explanation about your product, or do they need a testimonial that proves how great the product works? What motivates them into action?

If you don't know the answers, do some research. Find someone who represents your target, such as a current customer, and talk to them. Then sit down and write up a persona of your ideal target customer. Provide all the details. Create a persona or a set of personas that represent your target groups.

MISTAKE #4: RUSHING INTO PRODUCTION

You've read this far and know by now that preproduction is critical to a successful video launch, right? Give yourself plenty of time to do your video production right. Allow yourself some creative time to brainstorm and time to define the big picture of what you want to accomplish in the long term instead of jumping in and expecting fast results that will be impossible for your production team to deliver. Don't approach video marketing like one of my recent customers who asked me for filming dates and locations at the very start of preproduction, before anyone knew what the video would even be about. Skipping the basics can't be fixed after the fact—you need to have your strategies in place before you write the script, choose a production location, or schedule a shoot.

MISTAKE #5: JUMPING TO CONCLUSIONS

This happens a lot when people see the first results of their video implementation. They expect a video to go viral but only get 200 views and think it's a bomb. Instead of jumping to conclusions, use that information to improve results. Ask yourself questions to figure out what changes could improve your results: "Does my website have enough traffic? Is my video positioned well on my website? What about the thumbnail; does it invite people to click on it?" Maybe you need to fix your website or move the video to a different channel. If you've done everything right up to the launch, chances are that whatever you're not happy with can be adjusted and fixed.

MISTAKE #6: MAKING YOUR VIDEO TOO LONG

If you have the choice of making one five-minute video or three one-minute videos, go with the shorter videos. People won't hang around long enough to watch a long video. Those times are gone. Engage them quickly with a short, emotion- and value-driven video with a clear message and a call to action. Make three different ones to target groups at your three most critical points on the customer journey—where you need the most help, or where there is the greatest opportunity. Nowadays, five minutes is a very long time in this noisy world full of advertising.

MISTAKE #7: PUTTING TOO MANY MESSAGES IN YOUR VIDEO

The human brain can only absorb and retain so much in a short time. Choose one primary message and add a few minor ones—five total *max*. If you have a technical person on your team who wants to squeeze every fact, figure, number, and stat about your product into your one-minute video, encourage them to work with your web designer to create a page that has all that information—then create a simple, emotional video that gets people to your website where they can find that page if they need it!

MISTAKE #8: NOT BEING CLEAR WITH YOUR MESSAGE

This is one of the most common mistakes marketers make, and it's especially important to pay attention to with video. Talk the way your audience talks. Big words won't impress them and instead will drive them away.

People want to know what you're selling right away. Respect their time and make it clear within the first couple of seconds. Don't expect them to hang around for twenty seconds, like they've got nothing better to do. They do, and they will move on.

Be clear with the names of your company, product, and

service. You might think this is obvious, but unfortunately some companies come up with confusing names, thinking they'll be memorable. Words can't be memorable if people don't "get" them the first time. I've had this issue come up with businesses and tried to explain to them how important clarity is in their videos, but once they're stuck on a name, it's hard to convince them to change it.

MISTAKE #9: FORGETTING TO TELL A STORY

Facts fall away, but stories stick. Tell your viewers a story about what you do and who you do it for, and they will remember it. They might even remember some of the facts that you slid into the video. They will definitely remember how your video made them feel, especially if your story is emotional and targets them where they are on their customer journey and what they need to know right now.

MISTAKE #10: NOT GOING DEEP

Superficial videos fail to connect with people. Don't be afraid to get personal and tell people about why your company does what it does. Tell a story about your vision for the business, the product, and the customers you serve. Talk about a difficulty you encountered and how you overcame it to better understand your customers and deliver a better product. Show people that you genuinely *care*.

MISTAKE #11: FORGETTING ABOUT THE SOCIAL PROOF

Don't forget to put people in your videos. This can be a challenge for some businesses, but it's absolutely necessary. I worked with a rehab center whose clients did not want to appear in any of their marketing, but I knew that video of big empty rooms was not going to play well with the target audience. They needed *people*. In this case, we simply hired extras to populate the center. This made for a wonderful video with social proof of people enjoying all the activities and amenities the center offered.

MISTAKE #12: FORGETTING ABOUT DISTRIBUTION

People who get all excited about video production yet refuse to consider the importance of distribution set themselves up for failure. They might create a spectacular video, but when they put it on their website it only gets twenty views. It's like the saying "If a tree falls in the forest and there's no one around to hear it, did it make a sound?" If you make a video and there is no one around to see it, has it really been viewed? No, it has not.

MISTAKE #13: FOCUSING ON ONE CHANNEL

Start with your website, but plan to branch out to a multichannel strategy. Add one channel at a time and start testing and measuring the results. The world will not beat a path to your door if you don't create that path for it.

MISTAKE #14: NOT USING VIDEO SEO

Keywords, summaries, tags, subtitles, and all the other goodies that go into raising the ranking of your videos are easy to incorporate yet just as easy to overlook. Explore your channels' functions and work with your programmer or web developer to get all these set up correctly. Create a checklist for yourself so that every video you post follows best practices.

MISTAKE #15: EXPECTING RESULTS FROM JUST ONE VIDEO

Doing one video is not a waste, but it's just the first step in your video implementation. Your prospects and customers are at many different stages on their journey, and you can reach them at every stage with videos unique to them and their situations. Plan to add new videos on an ongoing basis for the best results. Don't miss out on the opportunity to attract people who are looking for exactly what you have to offer but haven't heard of you, and people who are making their buying decision today and have narrowed it down to you and one other competitor. These are huge markets that are ready-made for your business—if only they had a video to tell them that!

CONCLUSION

Video marketing is undervalued by many companies, to your advantage. You can easily separate yourself from the competition by using video marketing the right way.

This takes effort and a willingness to be vulnerable. You will be showing the face of your company, talking about your company, and talking about your motivations and your goals. You will have to be authentic to earn the trust of your audience, and you'll have to trust them to accept you.

Video marketing takes on a life of its own. Beyond the images, motion, and sounds, it allows you to touch people. Done right, video opens the door for people to trust you.

Any type of marketing has the ability to engage an audience, but video is different. You can transmit your message exactly the way you want it to be told, where you want it told, to the people who need to hear and see it. You can measure it and learn from the conclusions. In this way, you learn about your audience, too—they communicate to you with their views, likes, retweets, comments, and shares. That interaction lets you communicate with your market like never before. No other medium comes close to the power of video.

When YouTube began in 2005, no one realized where it would go or what it would become. Today it's the #2 search engine behind its parent company, #1 search engine Google. YouTube changed video marketing forever, and no one knows where it—and the plethora of other video platforms—will take us in the next decade.

When video marketing began, companies could put out videos that would be embarrassing by today's standards. They were inauthentic marketing pieces that didn't engage with audiences, and companies paid a small fortune to launch and distribute them.

Today, high-quality video marketing is available and affordable for just about every business. And the opportunities for reaching your customer have never been better. Whatever your target market, the people in that market probably have a phone with internet access and video capability in their pocket. People spend more time with their cell phones than they spend with their own family members—often, with their own children.

Video isn't just for selling. It's a way to grow your company authentically. You can't just throw anything out there in video and expect people to buy it. The market will let you know whether they like it—and your product or service—or not. You can use that feedback to figure out what your customers truly want and expect from you.

With video marketing, you can tell stories about your company's history, culture, products, services, mission, and vision. You can talk about your strengths and weaknesses—what you do better than anyone else, and where you're working to improve.

Video gives you the ability to change who you are and what your company stands for. To be truly authentic, it will force you to dig deep and remember why you built your company in the first place. It helps you get in touch with those roots, embrace them, and share them with your audience and invite that audience into your story with their own stories.

Welcome to video marketing. We have officially arrived, and we have so many places to go. Whether you're building an audience, launching your first video, or planning an entire video campaign, you're on the right track, and the possibilities are limitless. Jump in and get started. Show the world who you are and get to know your customers.

And remember to be yourself. That way you won't have to worry about copying what everyone else is doing. There is no company out there that's just like yours. When you're authentic, you are already the fresh new thing your audience is looking for.

Now it's time to show them what they want—with video marketing.

ACKNOWLEDGMENTS

I have the feeling that I can never be thankful enough. Throughout my journey to this book, I find countless people that I can call accountable. For the opportunities, belief, trust, feedback, and experiences that you gave me, thank you.

Mum and Dad: for your patience, time, love, and belief in me.

My wife, Paula: for the almost twenty years together through good and bad times, an amazing journey with always new adventures to go through and great stories to tell.

My son, Maxi: because of you, I am always looking forward to coming back home. I just enjoy every moment being with you (almost every moment, ha ha).

My family-in-law, Cris, Carlos, Mage, and Canyu Carranza: for accepting me as part of your family. Your support and inspiration mean a lot to me.

My team at youstream: this is just impossible without you! Special thanks to Reto Liesching for being a great business partner, videographer, and editor. To Alex R. Kaufmann for believing and trusting in our vision, and for all the crazy inspiring ideas. To Rafael Gschwend for bringing our business forward with outstanding stories and amazing motion graphics. To Matthias Strasser for delivering the graphics for this book. To Michelle Christen for your consistently great content that our customers love.

Florian Stein: without you I would have never discovered the power of SEO. You brought our company, our customers, and our expertise to the next level. It's always inspiring to talk to you, and I will always admire your strategic mind.

My editor, Susan Paul: it is just inspiring and fun working with you. Your interest in the topic, your smart questions, and your help made it a real pleasure to create this book.

My publishing manager, Kacy Wren: for your great support and keeping everything on schedule.

Scribe: I never have experienced a team with so much energy and dedication. You rock!

To our dear customers and business partners: you are all great contributors. From you I learn every day. We get thrown into projects, ideas, needs, and expectations from which we have the chance to try new things and live our creative drive.

Andreas Schneider: many years ago, you sparked the idea of doing all this. Thank you for your time, countless exciting conversations, and your support.

Christian Kemmer: for taking the time in the early days, teaching me about light settings and macro photography. You supported me on many occasions. I always look back on these moments with a lot of joy.

Leo Marty with the Universum team: your drive is amazing. Your belief in authentic video unites us. Thanks for the great and exciting projects!

Daniel Grob: for your great support on almost every topic and advice I need. I love your approach and the way you mentor me.

Hanspeter Muller: for being my first customer who is still a customer today. But most importantly, a great friend with whom I share many interests.

Andy Keel: for your friendship, for all the great entrepreneurial conversations, and for the exciting projects that started in the early days.

You, the reader: thank you for dedicating your time to reading this book. I hope you got some great takeaways that bring you and your business to the next level.

ABOUT THE AUTHOR

ADRIAN SANDMEIER is the founder and CEO of youstream, an award-winning video marketing company based in Switzerland.

He began his career in video with Swiss TV broadcaster tpc, working on national and international productions, including the Olympics.

For over a decade, his company youstream has helped hundreds of small- to mid-sized companies succeed. By producing video from social media spots and corporate films to explainer video and TV spots, Adrian has a unique insight that allows him to understand and communicate the big picture in video marketing to businesses and their audiences—their internal customers, partners, prospects, and customers. He advises countless marketing executives who approach him with questions like those answered in this book.

Adrian brings clarity to video marketing by overlaying it onto the customer journey and engaging his proven strategies for video marketing success. He believes the true power of video marketing lies in every link of the video strategy, beginning with a foundation built on trust, and carried through by addressing the right audience with a clear message and distribution that works.

Printed in Dunstable, United Kingdom